Creating Valuable Business Strategies

Creating Valuable Business Strategies

Shiv S. Mathur and Alfred Kenyon

AMSTERDAM • BOSTON • HEIDELBERG • LONDON
NEW YORK • OXFORD • PARIS • SAN DIEGO
SAN FRANCISCO • SINGAPORE • SYDNEY • TOKYO

Butterworth-Heinemann is an imprint of Elsevier

Butterworth-Heinemann is an imprint of Elsevier
Linacre House, Jordan Hill, Oxford OX2 8DP, UK
30 Corporate Drive, Suite 400, Burlington, MA 01803, USA

First edition 2008

British Library Cataloguing in Publication Data
A catalogue record for this book is available from the British Library

Library of Congress Cataloging-in-Publication Data
A catalog record for this book is available from the Library of Congress

For information on all Butterworth-Heinemann publications
visit our web site at books.elsevier.com

Printed and bound in Great Britain
08 09 10 10 9 8 7 6 5 4 3 2 1

ISBN: 978-0-7506-8548-1

Contents

Foreword

Mathur and Kenyon's *Creating Valuable Business Strategies* challenges current approaches to strategy analysis at a profound level. Their book also has important implications for the processes through which most companies develop their business strategies.

Their starting point is the marketplace. For all business enterprises this is where 'the rubber meets the road' – or, more precisely, where a business meets its customers and generates its revenues. An obvious place to start! Maybe. But this is not the point of departure for most current approaches to strategy-making or most books on strategic management. The more usual launching pads for strategy formulation are questions such as: 'What is your company's business?' 'Do you have a business model?' 'What industry are you in and what characterizes competition within it?' Mathur and Kenyon do not deny the importance of these questions. However, their approach is to view these more esoteric aspects of strategy within the context of the fundamental purpose of business: to create financial value by succeeding in customer markets. This rooting of strategic analysis in the firm's encounter with its customers leads to a critical discovery: the basic unit of strategy is the individual *offering* that customers choose or reject. That provides the foundation on which strategic analysis must build.

This starting point not only challenges many of our conventional tools and frameworks for strategy analysis, it also questions the approaches to strategy formulation used by most companies – especially the strategic planning systems which provide the formal structure for strategy-making within large corporations. Current approaches are primarily top-down. They start either with profit objectives ("To meet the stock market's expectations we need to grow earnings per share by 6% annually over the next three years"), or with strategic imperatives ordained by the CEO ("We will become the world's biggest and most admired supplier of moustache grooming products by the end of this decade.")

This is not to say that Mathur and Kenyon shun shareholder value objectives or the use of stretch goals as a management device – indeed, their whole analysis is built closely around the goal of growing the financial value of the firm. The critical difference is that, rather than beginning with the company's financial statements or with the CEO's profit targets and then working back, their focus is the starting point of the value creation process: designing and supplying an offering which customers prefer to competitors' rival offerings.

From this simple starting point, Mathur and Kenyon build an analysis which is both compelling in its logic and startling in terms of its contrasts with conventional strategy analysis. In particular, the analysis of competition they develop is strikingly different from the industry analysis popularised by Michael Porter. Once competition is viewed in terms of customer choices between rival offerings, prevailing notions of 'industry' are exposed as largely meaningless. The criterion of substitution not only reveals that many conventionally defined industries are irrelevant to most firms' strategic reality, it also means that markets need to be defined in relation to a specific offering. From the point of view of understanding competition, does the concept of a world watch industry make any sense? Does a watch produced by Patek Philippe compete with those supplied by Sekonda or Timex? The relevant market for a Patek Philippe watch is more likely to include offerings from suppliers of luxury jewellery rather than timepieces from mass-market watchmakers.

Viewing markets through the lens of the individual offerings offers new insight into strategic decisions. For example, it allows a more focused approach to differentiation, offers new tools for considering bundling decisions and lends itself to a systematic analysis of the basis of competitive advantage.

Unlike most business books, *Creating Valuable Business Strategies* is not limited to a single idea. At its foundation, of course, is the identification of the offering as the fundamental unit of strategy. However, from this foundation Mathur and Kenyon go on to build an analytic structure that is both internally consistent and comprehensive. Thus, while their analysis of markets and competition provides some of the most provocative and readily applicable parts of their analysis, they also ably integrate the critical role of resources into their framework. The comprehensiveness of the Mathur–Kenyon approach is revealed by its capacity to integrate decisions over positioning single offerings to the formulation of corporate strategy.

Companies that put Mathur and Kenyon's approach into action will see two major benefits. First, adopting a novel and rigorous approach to the delineation of markets and the analysis of competition and competitive advantage offers the potential for astute and innovatory strategic thinking. Second, an approach to value creation that begins with the realities of the marketplace offers the potential to extend their strategy-making process beyond the boardroom and the executive suite to embrace the important groups that in most firms are peripheral to strategy formulation – particularly those in marketing, sales and new product development.

Creating Valuable Business Strategies represents the successful integration of the micro-analysis of markets with value maximization by the firm. It is the fruit of interaction and debate between its co-authors – one an expert in strategic marketing, the other an expert in financial management – over many years. Their efforts have paid off.

Robert M. Grant
Professor of Management
McDonough School of Business
Georgetown University
Washington DC

Preface

With hindsight this book really began in the early 1980s with my attempt at designing a framework for competitive positioning. It was while discussing this framework with Alfred Kenyon – who had recently joined me at the City University Business School (now Cass Business School) after a long and distinguished career in industrial management – that the ideas described in this book began to be formed. Without the tremendous intellectual rigour and moral courage that Alfred brought to our partnership this book would never have been written. It was almost complete when Alfred passed away in March 2006.

The main idea behind this book now seems incredibly simple, and yet it was not immediately obvious. If, to be successful, a business must target profitable customers then what must be competitively positioned is what customers choose to buy, that is the offering. It is almost self-evident that what competes to be chosen by customers is the offering, not some bigger unit such as a profit centre, a division or the company itself. It took a little time for the penny to drop that there was a very strong case for making the individual offering the unit for competitive strategy.

Perhaps, what unconsciously delayed us was that using the offering as the strategic unit is a more radical departure from conventional approaches than might at first sight appear. Competitive strategies now need to be designed for many offerings, not for a handful of profit centres. The company's distinctive resources have to be discussed in the context of its many offerings. Moreover, corporate strategy must be recast as dealing with the company's collection of offerings, not profit centres. Strategy-making for many offerings clearly entails a much more intricate and untidy process than for a handful of profit centres. It is far too easy to fall into the trap of sacrificing reality at the altar of tidiness. We took some time to realize that the way forward was to tackle complexity, not to overlook it.

Alfred and I first presented our comprehensive approach to business strategy in our book *Creating Value* in 1997.[1] We were pleasantly surprised with the reception that it received. It won an award, many teachers and students used the book, and the ideas gained some currency with those managers to whom they were presented. The second revised edition was published in 2001.[2]

It was some time after that, that we began work on this book in earnest. In our terminology this is an entirely new offering. It is aimed firmly at practitioners. Our objectives are threefold. The first is to sharpen our ideas and hone them for practical use. The second is to communicate them in as clear a manner as we can, and without needlessly distracting managers with those arguments and references that would be of riveting interest only to academics. The third is to look at those companies who will have the most difficulty with our approach. We believe that these are mainly complex multi-unit companies in which the CEOs cannot personally be close to the various customer markets. We examine why top management in such companies may find our approach irksome and what can be done to resolve these tensions, and why that is important.

It is a pleasure to acknowledge the enormous support that we received in the writing of this book.

Some friends provided powerful help. Paul Raimond read through an entire draft and made some very useful suggestions. David Citron helped by checking some of the financial reasoning we put forward. Robert Grant has for many years encouraged us by discussing and commenting on our unconventional ideas.

Joan Kenyon made an enormous contribution. Alfred was determined to finish this book and often wrote while in great pain from an incurable cancer. Joan, his wife, was his constant carer.

My wife Shobha made it possible for me to write by keeping the world at bay. I received a lot of help from my son Tarun in verifying some facts and in providing some modern and telling illustrations. My daughter Rittu, many years ago, had encouraged me enormously by saying that the idea that companies competed via their offerings was so obvious that it should be labelled 'the kindergarten theory of strategy'.

Our editor at Elsevier, Maggie Smith, made the logistical task of publication almost painless.

After Alfred passed away, I alone put the finishing touches to this book. No doubt I have added numerous errors. I now alone must take responsibility for all mistakes.

Finally, I should like to record how much these ideas have been part of Alfred's and my life for over two decades and how much I enjoyed pursuing them together. It is one of the most pleasant things I have ever done.

Shiv Mathur

Notes

1. Mathur, S.S. and Kenyon, A. (1997). *Creating Value: Shaping Tomorrow's Business.* Oxford: Butterworth Heinemann.
2. Mathur, S.S. and Kenyon, A. (2001). *Creating Value: Successful Business Strategies.* Second edition. Oxford: Butterworth Heinemann.

Executive summary: The framework outlined

- This book is about business strategy which it sees as consisting of:
  a. competitive strategy which designs an individual future offering
  b. corporate strategy which manages a company's future collection of offerings by deciding which offerings to add, retain or divest.
- It sees strategy in terms of offerings because the most important decisions about our business are made not by any of us, but by our customers. They choose or reject what we offer to sell them: our offerings. To be successful, we must therefore target profitable customers with competitively attractive offerings.
- Competitive strategy manages the design of an individual future offering which will generate value for us tomorrow. We must design our offering in such a way that customers will choose to buy it, rather than those that compete with it.
- An offering will build value if its cash flows exceed those that earn its cost of capital. It must do that long enough to pay back the cash originally invested before the offering was launched. Value-building cash flows must therefore be durable enough to outlast that payback period.
- To achieve that, an offering must be designed to do two things:
  a. to occupy a winning competitive position and
  b. to exploit one or more of our own company's winning resources.
  Both are needed, like the twin blades of a pair of scissors.
- The object of business, and the reason why cash is invested in it, is to build value. It is not some social or ecological objective, as is argued by advocates of the stakeholder view, nor is it to get bigger, nor is it risk diversification. A business is only 'born' if investors believe it will produce value, and it 'dies' when investors no longer believe that.

- Ethical conduct of business is, however, desirable for many reasons. For the most part it helps the value objective. In any case, managers are human beings with ethical value systems.
- However, the business itself is not an ethical agent; it is an inanimate investment project.
- The first of our two requirements for a value-building offering is a winning competitive position. The fundamental choice here is whether we wish to compete on price or by differentiation.
- Our preference might be for price competition if we have a sustainable unit cost advantage.
- A differentiated offering is one which more closely matches the preferences of a targeted group of customers. More closely than competing substitutes.
- Customers receive better value for which they are willing to pay above the market price charged for substitutes. The size of that price premium measures the achieved degree of differentiation. What matters is the perceptions of customers, not any intrinsic features of the offering.
- With differentiated offerings customers compare not prices, but value for money.
- The advantage of differentiation to the seller is the degree of extra freedom to set prices. Within the premium that customers are willing to pay, we can go for less margin and greater volume or more margin and less volume, whichever is most profitable to ourselves.
- Differentiation is a powerful tool for positioning offerings in their markets. We can differentiate in various dimensions and to any low or high degree. A particularly powerful choice is that between the *support* and the *merchandise* dimensions. Support for this purpose means help with choosing, obtaining and using the offering. Merchandise is the word used for all other differentiating features. Each of these main dimensions has subdimensions. The upshot is a rich vein of different customer preferences that we can meet with our new offering.
- In modern times most offerings are differentiated. They do not compete in wider 'industries', but each in a more or less distinct *private* market, not wholly shared with any other offering.
- Many markets are not fully competitive in the sense that any offering can enter and compete on equal terms. This is because they

are dominated by one firm or by a dominant group of firms. In such dominated markets, as in others, offerings may or may not be differentiated. Dominated markets present different threats and opportunities and suit some companies better than others. Strategists must bear these differences in mind when deciding to enter or stay out.

- Our company's winning resources are what enable our attractively positioned offerings to beat their competition: to generate better value both for our customers and our company, and to sustain this excellence throughout the payback period.
- A resource is a winning one if it has all four of these cornerstones: it must be *distinctive*, a *bargain*, *matchless* and *inseparable*. Distinctive means unique to our company, bargain means that we must not pay the whole of its value to us in order to acquire it, matchless means that others must not be able to acquire a resource which produces offerings with the same attraction as ours. Inseparable means that others must not be able to poach the resource; nor must employees or suppliers who carry the resource be able to appropriate its value by holding us to ransom.
- Winning resources can be of many kinds, but they are often hard to recognize and embedded in collective skills and routines. These characteristics help to make them matchless and inseparable.
- Corporate strategy manages not single offerings, but the company's entire collection of offerings. It constantly seeks to enhance the value of the collection by additions or divestments. Checking whether offerings should be divested is one of its most significant tasks. Companies tend to retain offerings beyond the point where they build value.
- The addition of offerings is known as 'diversification'. Diversification can build value only if it is *related*. In other words if the new offering has some commonality or link with the rest of the company: relatedness is not a matter of belonging to the 'same' industry. There are seven such links. The need for relatedness is heavily stressed because the track record of unrelated diversification has been so disastrous in the past.
- In fact, in much of the twentieth century there was a great rush for diversification, mainly with the mistaken objective of increasing the size of the company. Most of this was unsuccessful. Hence corporate

strategy needs to apply some stringent criteria: a better-off test and three filters to new diversification proposals.

- The better-off test simply tests whether the new offering will build value. Relatedness is regarded as a condition of passing it. The filters are a corrective for the optimism that may allow unsuitable propositions to slip through the test.
- The filters are the best-owner filter, the robustness filter and the market-instead filter. The best-owner filter checks that our company is the best owner of the new offering; that it would not be more valuable in other hands. The robustness filter checks that the new offering adds value even in adverse future conditions. The market-instead filter checks that the benefit of the new offering could not be obtained by market contract; it concerns proposals for vertical integration.
- Retain-or-divest decisions use the same criteria, except that they do not need the robustness filter. Valuation is at the date of the review, not that of the original investment decision.
- The offering-based approach to strategy advocated in this book causes strain within many companies, especially complex companies. This is because day-to-day management is usually and for good reasons structured in much wider units, such as profit centres or even divisions. Organizational units are designed largely for internal tasks; offerings by contrast need to be shaped with an eye on external parties: customers and competitors. These diverging orientations cause conflict and the offering can get lost in that structure. Our answer is to give each offering a sponsor to oversee its progress from design to approval to implementation and finally to monitoring its performance till it has ceased to add value and is divested. Sponsors can combine this task with other functions if necessary, and will normally sponsor a number of offerings each, depending on the weight of the individual offerings.
- To sum up the book asks 'what should be our future offerings?' as its prime strategic question and presents a framework to help managers answer it. A framework that applies to businesses large or small, domestic or international.

Introduction

Introduction: The Book in Outline

Yet another book on business strategy? Well, we hope the reader will find this one different.

This book does not see strategy as

- something easy or simple, like the gimmick of the month;
- dramatic restructuring or mergers;
- big and traumatic shake-ups of large organizations, like Exxon, Unilever or General Electric;
- just pleasing or persuading customers;
- just internal cost control; and
- just having the right people in the right jobs.

In this book the centrepiece of strategy is the 'offering'. That term is a convenient one embracing both 'product' and 'service', and also all the sales efforts and supporting activities that customers consider when they choose to buy.[1] Strategy we see as the design of future offerings.[2] The flip side of designing a new offering for sale tomorrow is the search for sustainably profitable customers who will be attracted to that new offering, and choose it against competing rival offerings.

This new perspective has a number of consequences that help to make this book different:

- Strategy is a task for all businesses with offerings, even the smallest, not just for giants.
- Strategy is about customers because they are *choosers*. It is no good pleasing customers if they do not choose our offering. Their choices are our targets.

- Strategy is also, however, about us and our strong points. Customers will not sustainably remain profitable for us unless our company is the best provider of our proposed new offering.

Finally, this book unashamedly holds that the object of strategy is the creation of financial value. We have no politically correct illusions about the primacy of 'stakeholders', nor do we aim at growth for growth's sake. Business has only one objective: value creation. Those who direct and manage a business should do it fairly and ethically, but the objective is value.[3]

The book is therefore specially addressed to anyone who plays a part in designing and choosing the future offerings of the business.

We develop this agenda in six stages: Part 1 sets the scene. Part 2 describes how an offering is competitively positioned vis-à-vis rival offerings and customers, Part 3 discusses winning resources and why offerings need them, Part 4 corporate strategy, that is the managing of the company's whole collection of offerings, and Part 5 the implications for organizing and structuring for an offering-centred approach to strategy. Part 6 deals with those aspects of this new framework which tend to meet with resistance. It explores why they are stumbling-blocks, and what can be learned from that.

Parts 2 and 3 therefore deal with competitive strategy, which is for a single offering, whereas Part 4 deals with corporate strategy, which is for the collection as a whole.

Notes

1. Mathur, S.S. (1992). Talking straight about competitive strategy. *Journal of Marketing Management*, **8**, 199–217. Also see Anderson, J.C., Carpenter, G.S. and Narus, J.A. (2001). Managing market offerings in business markets. In: D. Iacobucci (ed.) *Kellogg on Marketing*. New York: Wiley, pp. 330–365.
2. Kenyon, A. and Mathur, S.S. (2002). The offering as the strategic focus. *Journal of Strategic Marketing*, **10**, 171–188.
3. Sternberg, E. (1995). *Just Business*. London: Warner Books.

PART 1

Setting the Scene

Part 1 deals with the basics of this framework for business strategy. Chapter 1 introduces the framework and sets out why it focuses on the design of future offerings rather than larger units. Chapter 2 makes the case for financial value as the object of business and discusses rejected alternative objectives, such as 'growth' or the stakeholder view. Chapter 3 sets out the fundamental view taken of how a successful offering needs to be designed, with both a winning competitive position and the employment of winning resources.

1

The need to design future offerings

Managers are bombarded with advice on strategy, but what do they really think strategy is about? Perhaps the ideas in circulation contain any or even all of the following topics:

- structuring companies for success;
- leadership;
- corporate governance;
- relations with investors and other stakeholders;
- growth, market share, acquisitions;
- financial control of costs and capital investment;
- investment project analysis;
- technology and innovation; and
- marketing.

'Strategic' has almost become an attribute of any topic of interest to managers or writers.

This book seeks to focus the agenda on the creation of financial value, which it sees as the fruit of identifying, attracting and satisfying profitable customers. This requires two main tasks:

1. finding promising customer markets and
2. exploiting the company's own excellence in any such market.

Only in combination can these two efforts create value.

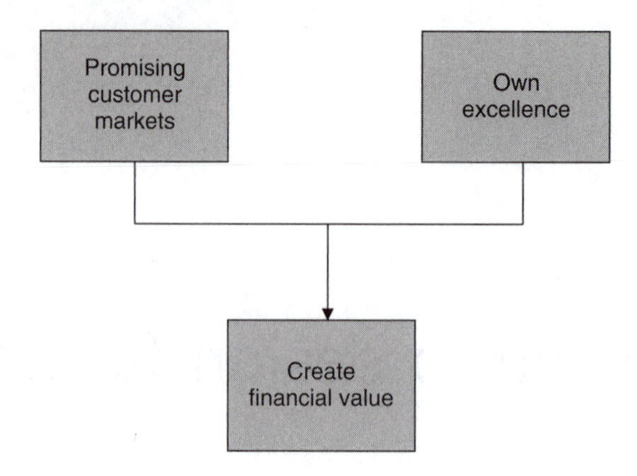

Figure 1.1 Creating financial value

The first of these tasks concerns issues *outside* the business, and the second issues *inside* the business. The decisive trick is to choose external markets that fit and exploit our internal points of excellence, as in Figure 1.1.[1]

This agenda differs from the assorted topics in the above list and also from other current doctrines in three important ways:

1. Its more explicit focus on value.
2. Its much greater attention to choosing customers. Success depends on their choices.
3. Its balanced and targeted treatment of internal, non-marketing issues.

This approach differs from what we might call the managerialist one which seeks to treat strategy as far as possible as an inward-facing task: striving for excellence in manufacturing, R&D, operational efficiency, quality control and so on. We must also, however, dissociate it from the opposite approach, that is the extreme marketing one. This extreme marketing view appears to err in two respects:

1. It concentrates on customers to the exclusion of internal tasks, problems and opportunities.
2. It sees customers as practically the only focus of attention, but without stressing their key role as *choosers*.

This last view is of course the extreme, but not uncommon marketing view: more balanced writers and practitioners of marketing do not fall into either of these traps. However, marketing must always fall short of total business strategy as long as it fails to provide a complete guide to sustained value creation. Our task in this book is just that.

There is another important difference. Strategy is usually, but not here, tackled as though the business world consisted entirely of multi-unit companies, too complex for the head office or CEO to have intimate knowledge of the customers and markets served. Small and simple businesses are tacitly assumed to face the same strategic issues as large and complex ones. In complex companies that intimate knowledge of customers and markets resides in middle managers, who do not have the power to make the ultimate decisions about resource allocations or the company's activities. Knowledge of markets and top direction are in separate hands.

Such complex businesses are not, however, the only kind of business. There exists a multitude of mainly small businesses, where a single entrepreneur operates in customer markets and in the internal resources and logistics that serve those markets. One person has both tasks. We call them 'simple' companies.

In this book we tackle the strategic task faced by any company with offerings. The additional difficulties of complex companies are of course addressed as extra issues. After all, not all companies can be simple. We do, however, stress the advantages of simplicity. There are those who passionately argue that 'small is beautiful'.[2] We add that simple is beautiful, too.

In fact, the current fashion is to treat the topic of business strategy as mainly concerning the leadership and other qualities of the top managers, especially those in large and complex companies. That is a topic of critical importance. It is also validly treated as 'strategy', in the sense that it is what many people mean by that word. That, however, is not the original meaning of 'strategy', which is a metaphor taken from a military context. A brilliant general like Napoleon at Austerlitz prepares for a battle by disposing his forces so as to surprise the enemy and to exploit the weak points in the enemy's deployment. It is those dispositions and plans, and not his leadership qualities, that represent the military usage of the word 'strategy'. We are not using the word in that leadership sense.

Value is Created in Offerings

The purpose of business is to create financial value, that is to earn returns in excess of the cost of capital (see Chapter 2). A commercial business generates financial value in its customer markets. Hence those who run a company or a part of one should constantly be asking what it should be marketing to customers in the future, either along with present offerings or after those have reached their sell-by date.

The thing that is marketed to customers is an *offering*. That word includes both tangible 'products' and intangible 'services' and also the sales efforts and supporting activities that shape customer choice. We now apply the pattern in Figure 1.1 to each offering. Each new offering must create financial value for the company. To achieve that, it must meet two conditions as in Figure 1.2:

1. It must occupy a winning competitive position.
2. It must depend on one or more of the company's very own winning resources.

We shall encounter Figure 1.2 again in Chapter 10, which discusses the scissors process.

Both these conditions must be met. They are firmly linked like the two blades of the pair of scissors in Figure 1.2. Much of the book will set out just what it takes to find a 'winning' competitive position or again a 'winning' resource. Both are rare and take some finding.

A manager who reads this may wonder why we ascribe winning characteristics to just two features: the competitive position and winning resources. What about all the things that managers worry about all day long: cost effectiveness, inventory control, the supply chain, employee relations, sales and distribution management, credit control,

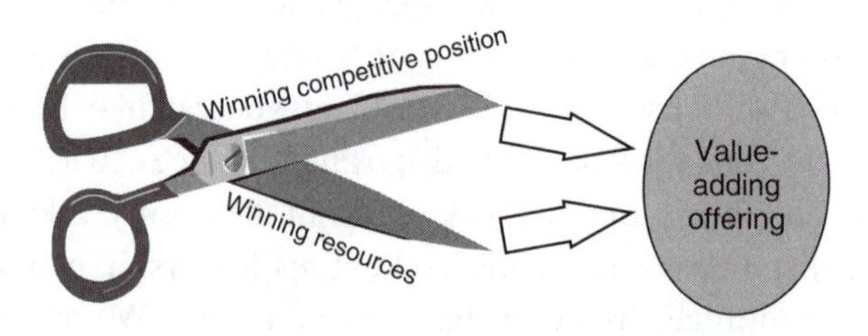

Figure 1.2 The scissors – the two conditions for value-adding offerings

and all the other tasks of good management? Well, those topics concern day-to-day management, which includes the task of *implementing* strategies. This book is mainly about designing, selecting and planning a winning future offering. That strategic task is of course incomplete without the implementation process, and for that reason we discuss the implications of the offering-based approach for the task of implementation in Part 5. However, our central and pivotal strategic task is the identification and design of winning future offerings.

In this book a single competitive strategy concerns the design of an individual future offering. The company therefore needs as many competitive strategies as it has offerings.

Most businesses have more than one offering, some have thousands. They must not only design individual new offerings, but also constantly monitor the composition of their list of offerings as a whole. They must ask which of them need to be removed from the list, and what new ones would add value. Part 4 deals with managing the totality of the company's offerings. That task we call *corporate strategy.*

The book therefore asks, 'what should be our future offerings?' as its primary strategic question. We do not suggest that the answer is easy. However, the book is dedicated to it.

A Significant Question

We therefore hope to help our reader to make decisions about offerings to add or divest. Our company competes for customers with its offerings. No offering has an infinite life. Hence if we wish to stay in business, we must keep developing new future offerings.

Any decision to market a new offering is a *strategic* decision. It commits us to an objective, and to a way to attain it. It chooses a market to contest, for what customers and against what competitors. It updates or redefines our future place or places in the world of business. Each such decision also closes some alternative options.

Why This Decision?

There are many other strategic decisions, such as what business we are in, what facilities we need, or how we should structure our company for dealing with customers and other outside parties. However, decisions about offerings to add or divest are second to none of them in importance. These other questions face inwards at our own organization. Our question in this book is about our future place in our environment, in our markets.

At the same time, even if the other decisions are no more important than ours, they too are nevertheless important and strategic. Any decision is strategic if the answer to it commits our whole company to move in certain directions, and closes some options to move in other directions.

Non-strategic Questions and Answers

These reflections are not startling, but managers have been known to use the big word 'strategy' for some smaller decisions. There was the managing director of a medium-sized company who said his strategy was 'to move the factory' to a location some 10 miles from the current one. One hears of 'strategies' designed to save tax, perhaps by changing the group of companies' legal structure. Such decisions do not in their own right change the business of the company. They are important, but not direction changing. We shall not call them strategic, nor do we see that usage as helpful.

Again, we prefer not to treat as strategic any decisions that would not face a simple or small business. A shoe repairer – a sole trader in more than one sense – is not concerned with how much responsibility should be delegated to subsidiary companies, divisions or profit centres. Shoe repairers have no such sub-units, only customers and suppliers. They too, however, must identify their markets, that is their customers and competitors. For example, should they repair orthopaedic footwear, a task needing more skill and time? Our concept of strategy applies to any size of business, however small.

There are also some gimmick uses of the word 'strategy' which express passing fads and fashions. As Nigel Piercy puts it in his book *Market-led Strategic Change*, strategy is about:[3]

> Breaking free from an obsession with *management tools* that are spectacular and seductive in improving operational efficiency, but are not strategy – such as total quality management, benchmarking, time-based competition, outsourcing, re-engineering, lean supply chain management, efficient consumer response, and so on – on the grounds that while

> operational effectiveness and strategy are both essential to superior performance, operational effectiveness does not substitute for strategic direction.

These nuts-and-bolts tasks fail to cover what customers might want to buy from us, rather than from our competitors, at profitable combinations of price and volume. Other so-called 'strategies' such as 'delighting customers' make the opposite mistake of designing what customers will certainly buy, but with no thought given to whether it will make money. There is no surer way of delighting customers than to charge nothing.

So if you, reader, want to find some magic single trick which will make your company rich, do not read on! You will not find it here. Successful strategy is a matter of commonsense, but it is not simple.

Why the Offering?

In this book we ask where to compete next, and by that we mean what offerings we should market next. However, why design each offering separately? Could we not instead develop goals for a 'product' range, or for a whole profit centre?

As mentioned earlier, the word 'offering' simply means what a customer chooses to buy, be it a physical 'product' or an intangible 'service'. Moreover, when customers choose a particular washing machine or refrigerator or PC, they are not just choosing the box and its contents, but all the before- and after-sales service, warranties, brand reputation and the like that they perceive to be surrounding that box. It is that totality that customers choose.

An offering is something bought by customers with a price that customers can compare. Each of the company's offerings has a unique competitive position vis-à-vis customers and competing substitutes.

As the customer is the arbiter of success, we have to design what that customer will compare with competing substitutes before choosing. Seeing our company's future in terms of offerings is not an option, but an unavoidable commitment. It may not be the only way to look at the future, but it is not optional either. Customers decide the fate of a business in competitive markets. That is why offerings have to be designed for how they will appear to customers comparing them with nearby substitutes, and why the task of designing them is so critical to success.

Some objections answered

The idea that what we must design is individual offerings is at odds with conventional approaches to business strategy, and there are a number of objections to it, which we shall now examine.[4]

Convenience

Let us not pretend that the offering is a convenient strategic unit. It is seldom a natural management unit or profit centre. Worse, in many companies offerings are numerous. There is no doubt that strategy-making for offerings imposes extra cost and effort in complex companies. The handful of profit centres would make significantly cheaper and tidier units. The offering as the unit therefore has significant drawbacks. Yet the fact remains that customers choose offerings, not profit centres, and that no competitive strategy can succeed unless it produces customer choices that build value for us.

Resources, not offerings sway customer choices

Some objectors regard resources, rather than customer choices, as the central issue. They point to a company like Canon, claiming that Canon's preeminence in photo-imaging gives it such a near-monopoly in that field as to make the resource decisive irrespective of the individual offerings.[5] The contention is that customers have no attractive alternatives, due to the decisive effect of the company's resource. Similarly, if Wal-Mart has capabilities which enable it to offer significantly lower prices than other supermarkets, is that not enough to win over many of those competitors' customers?

The Canon case is a strong one, because it comes close to a monopoly, in this case driven by leadership in technology. Objectors argue from cases like this that winning customers is merely an important fruit of deploying the necessary winning resources. That deployment is regarded as enough to ensure success with customers. The fact is that monopoly kills customers' freedom to choose, at least in the short run. In the longer run, market forces will attract competitors of one sort or another. As long as a monopoly lasts, the importance of customers' choices is severely reduced, but even then they cannot be completely neglected. In any case customers' preferences often shift autonomously, without any action by us or by our competitors. In many countries preferences have moved away from tobacco products, from animal furs and from spectacles like cockfighting. Even in Canon's extreme case it is perilous to see competitive issues exclusively in terms of matters internal to the supplier, such as resources. Customers are hardly ever so completely captive that the seller can afford to ignore their possible reactions. More importantly, cases where customers are completely captive will always be exceptions, and probably short-lived exceptions, not the rule. Normally customers can choose to buy from others.

The Wal-Mart case is much weaker, because it concerns simply what was at its peak a strong competitive position in a highly competitive business. There is no monopoly, and customers have choices. Moreover, customers may even come to resent such dominance by one seller, for example by boycotting Wal-Mart's stores or blocking its real estate applications on environmental grounds, as has occurred in California.

To sum this up, if we know what is good for us, we can never forget about customers. Seller's markets do occur, but they are rare and unlikely to persist for long.

Customers do not choose individual offerings, but wider units

Finally, there are objectors who accept that competitive strategy is about winning the choices of customers, but maintain that customers choose a brand, or a product range, or a comfort factor, and therefore the company or business unit or profit centre rather than the offering. Gillette may serve as an example of a brand. An example of a range is where an airline buys all its aircraft from the same manufacturer. An example of a comfort factor is where a company consults PricewaterhouseCooper for tax advice, rather than a less substantial and less well-known firm in a provincial town. Yet in all those cases it is still the offering that customers choose. The brand, range or comfort factor has no price that the customer can compare with the price of rival substitutes. Brands, ranges and comfort factors are important *features* of offerings. They can play a big role in shaping customers' perceptions and choices, but none of them are *what* is chosen. Customers do not, for example, buy brands, but branded offerings. Nor do they buy reputation, just reputable offerings.

Heinz illustrates the brand argument. Heinz successfully marketed baked beans early in the twentieth century. Their slogan for many years was '57 varieties', although that number was soon exceeded. They established a strong brand image, and exploited that with many other offerings such as tomato ketchup and other sauces and food products. As a brand strategy it was successful. Shoppers find the brand an attractive feature of Heinz offerings, but not necessarily a decisive one. They do not invariably buy the name Heinz regardless of price and other competitive features of competing substitutes. Shoppers still choose between offerings, not between brands. If Heinz baked beans are out of stock, they choose another brand: they do not buy Heinz salad cream instead.

For a few years at the turn of the twenty-first century only one mobile telephone maker was clearly seen to create financial value: Nokia. Some others failed because their offerings were not sufficiently attractive to users to earn their keep. Whether our company succeeds or fails depends on the choices of customers, and customers do not choose *ranges* of offerings, let alone the collective outputs of entire profit centres. Even though Nokia offered several models of mobile phones ranging from the ordinary to the elaborate, it was not the *range* that competed. Each model competed with its nearest non-Nokia substitutes. Even if a customer, at ease with Nokia's operating system, chose between two of its phones, that choice concerned the offering, not the range. Companies can offer product ranges but customers choose offerings. Customers choose and pay for an individual offering, something with a price and other features which they can compare with those of competing offerings.

To sum this up, we have to design what customers choose, and that is the offering. If our offerings do not create value, the company must fail.

The Simple Case for Needing Both a Winning Position and a Winning Resource

This following simple illustration about business consultancy merely serves to show why both the winning position and the winning resource are needed. It will not describe either of them in adequate detail.

The turn of the third millennium saw a lot of management and professional redundancies, because downsizing and outsourcing had become a fashionable response to recession. Consequently many of those who became redundant, considered setting up as self-employed business consultants. The snag was that so many tried to break into that field. It became oversupplied. Nevertheless business management was the only skill that many redundant managers could hope to exploit.

So how would Phoebe set about finding a profitable consultancy practice?

Commonsense would suggest that she should find a niche which both needed her own special skills and talents and was located in a growth area.

As it happened, Phoebe's main experience was in mergers and acquisitions. However, in a recession that skill was hardly in buoyant demand. On the other hand, the period around 2000 was a growth period for attention to social responsibility and other ethical concerns. So was the skill of managing redundancies, or that of outsourcing. So these and others were clearly candidates worthy of Phoebe's consideration. However, Phoebe's experience in setting up mergers and acquisitions had given her little practical contact with handling redundancies. She was not likely to be a winning competitor here. On the other hand, she may well have had a lot of contact with social responsibility issues, and have some superior skills in that area. So that might be one of the offerings in which she might be able to combine a promising competitive position with a winning resource. She needs to go for something both in lively demand and also in need of her very own special skills and experience.

The combination of these two prerequisites is mere commonsense, not a far-fetched counsel of perfection.

Do We Need to be Customer-Centred?

There is much wrangling over whether managers should be customer-centred, and it is sometimes objected that to treat the offering as the unit of strategy is 'unbalanced', in that it overplays the importance of customers and underplays that of the company's own strengths and weaknesses.[6]

Our approach is customer-centred in the sense that we are against taking any big decisions without heeding their impact on our ability to attract profitable customers. However, we are middle-of-the-road in suggesting that a successful future offering must meet two tests. It must both (a) occupy a winning competitive position and (b) use one or more of the company's own winning resources. Neither the demand nor the supply side can be ignored.

We are not of course customer-centred in the sense of thinking that the purpose of a business is to delight customers.

What Gives Customers Special Importance?

Do customers in fact present a different challenge from other important partners of the business, like employees or suppliers? They do in one way. Customers choose us: we choose the others.

This book therefore gives a high priority to the need to plan for customer choices. However, it does not give customers priority over investors. Financial success is the primary goal of strategy. Chapter 2 deals with that. However, financial success has to be achieved in customer markets. It is in that context that the book is customer-centred.

Implications of the Offering as the Strategic Unit

To use the offering as the strategic unit is a more radical departure than might at first sight appear. The normal thrust of strategy advice deals with internal structures and capabilities. It may even 'position' the company or a business unit as being more concerned with either quality or differentiation or lower unit costs than competitors,[7] but all this focuses on the seller vis-à-vis its competitors, not on customers and their choices. What customers choose is offerings, not companies or their units. Our offering-centred approach here stands that normal thrust on its head. The desired effect in customer markets is central, and the internal implications become instrumental to that.

The practical implications are enormous. Resources are central to strategy, but they are seldom specific to just one offering. Hence *decisions* about new offerings often have to be not just for each offering, but also for any other offerings, present and future, that might be affected because they share this or that resource. The decision may thus have

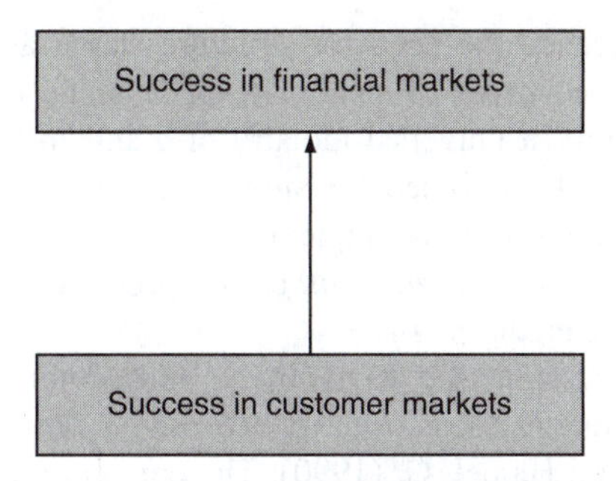

Figure 1.3 The fundamental business objective and its source

to be about several offerings. It is the *design* that has to deal separately with each offering and its position. Again, corporate strategy has to deal not with the company's collection of profit centres or business units,[8] but with its collection of offerings. Takeovers, demergers and other big transactions are treated as steps in the management of the collection of *offerings*.

These changes do not make strategy easier or cheaper to frame. They do, however, focus the strategist's mind on customer markets, in which the goal of financial success has to be achieved. This is illustrated in Figure 1.3.

Summary

The strategic question to be examined in this book is the design of new future offerings. There are other strategic questions that should also be asked, but this one is at least no less important than the others. An offering is only likely to add financial value to the company if it occupies a winning competitive position, and also depends on one or more winning resources. To find such an offering is not easy, but there are no simple shortcuts to strategic success.

Notes

1. This idea of internal and external fit in itself is not new; see Andrews, K.R. (1971). *The Concept of Corporate Strategy*. Homewood, Illinois: Irwin.
2. Schumacher, E.F. (1993). *Small is Beautiful.* London: Vintage Books. Schumacher's ideas were not as dogmatic as the title of his book may

suggest. He conceded the need for structures large and small. However, he insisted on 'the virtues of smallness' because he felt that '[t]oday we suffer from an almost universal idolatry of giantism' (p. 49). Our phrase 'simple is beautiful' is coined for similar reasons, that is to counter the prevailing tendency towards complexity.

3. Piercy, N. (1997). *Market-led Strategic Change*. Second edition. Oxford: Butterworth Heinemann, p. 141.
4. For a fuller discussion, see Kenyon, A. and Mathur, S.S. (2002). The offering as the strategic focus. *Journal of Strategic Marketing*, **10**, 171–188.
5. Prahalad, C.K. and Hamel, G. (1990). The core competence of the corporation. *Harvard Business Review*, May–June.
6. For a version of this argument, see Finlay, P. (2000). *Strategic Management*. Harlow: Financial Times Prentice Hall, pp. 174–175.
7. Porter, M.E. (1980). *Competitive Strategy*. New York: Free Press.
8. As is usually portrayed by writers on strategy. See, Porter, M.E. (1985). *Competitive Advantage*. New York: Free Press. See also, Goold, M., Campbell, A. and Alexander, M. (1994). *Corporate-level Strategy*. New York: Wiley.

2

The purpose of a business is to build value

What is a business for? Why was it formed in the first place? What is the difference between success and failure? We suggest that a business exists to generate long-term financial value for its investors.

If that makes the reader yawn, it is understandable. It has become a commonplace. However, yawns may be premature.

In this chapter we first give 'value' a precise and practical meaning, and set out the criteria that should be applied. The chapter then describes and discusses the main objection to value as the objective, made by those who prefer the stakeholder view of what business is for. We clarify that in rejecting the stakeholder view we do not advocate that business managers should act unethically or even uncaringly. Although the stakeholder view has found favour with a number of senior managers, few of its originators and principal advocates have experienced the decisions and dilemmas that face practising managers. Because the stakeholder approach still causes so much discussion in the early years of the twenty-first century, we give it a thorough airing.

The chapter then discusses two alternative objectives which are popular with managers rather than with outsiders: risk diversification and size. Neither of these is necessarily believed by its champions to be incompatible with the means of achieving value. We state our reasons for rejecting all these and other alternative objectives, leaving value creation as the sole aim.

Just What is Financial Value?

Managers are familiar with the normal discounted cash flow (DCF) evaluation technique for ascertaining the net present value (NPV) of a project.[1] The NPV is what we mean by financial value. The technique is commonly used to evaluate a new project. In our view a business comes into being as a project. Similarly, new offerings are projects. The NPV of a new offering is the sum of the expected future cash flows of the investment and other expenditures and the revenues expected to flow from them, discounted to the present day at the discount rate which takes account of the degree of risk of this particular offering. That discount rate is also what we call its cost of capital. If the offering has a positive NPV, it passes the test: it generates value. In the decision to invest in a new offering the zero date to which the cash flows are discounted is always the date of that decision.

Financial value is therefore *created* by cash flows in excess of those that earn the cost of capital. The NPV is here the financial value of a project, such as a new offering at the date of the decision to invest in it.

Decisions to invest or not to invest are made by investors or on behalf of investors. Financial value therefore starts from the viewpoint of investors. Investors include of course lenders as well as owners. The value of the business to owners can be improved by giving the company an optimum level of debt. This is also an optimal leverage, where leverage (or gearing) means the ratio of debt to equity. However, leverage is an issue of funding, of financial management, and that is not our concern in this book. We here simply define financial value as being value to owners or shareholders.

Financial Value and Profit

Financial value is related to, but distinct from, profit. Financial value uses cash flows, that is receipts and payments as its raw material. Profit on the other hand is the excess of income over expenditure, both defined in accounting terms. This accounting concept has the following shortcomings for the purpose of evaluating new projects:[2]

1. Profit (or loss) relates to one period (e.g. a year) at a time, and cannot be related to all the cash flows out and in over the lifetime of the project.
2. Profit does not measure the time value of money, as does NPV. The time value of money recognizes that cash returns in year 5 are not as valuable as those in year 4.
3. Income and expenditure are not cash concepts, whereas investment is a cash event. Returns to an investment can only be measured in cash flows, not in accrual terms including depreciation and other provisions, which serve the purpose of allocating income and expenditure to appropriate accounting periods.
4. The accounting measurement of profit often requires subjective judgements at the end of each period, such as inventory valuations, doubtful debt provisions and the like. Cash receipts and payments do not.
5. Profit tends to be contrasted with loss, implying a performance yardstick of zero profit. Financial value's yardstick or hurdle is the expected rate of return, that is the cost of capital. Its threshold level is therefore at a point above zero profit. A positive rate of return, which falls short of the cost of capital, represents a *loss* of financial value.

Ratios like return on capital employed (ROCE) or return on sales (ROS) are indispensable as control ratios for overall results in a given accounting period. Such control ratios need to be accounting ratios, as only accounting data are available. However, they are inappropriate for assessing a new project, like a new offering, where the critical hurdle is its zero NPV.

Financial Value: An Illustration

On Legless Paradise Island in the Pacific Ocean there were two brewers of lager beers, Merry and Tipsy. Merry was the larger of the two with a strong brand and a strong position with retailers, until Tipsy fought back with a licence to produce alcotrops. These alcoholic drinks incorporated tropical fruit juices and were very popular with younger

Table 2.1 Merry's options

	Lager sales	Alcotrop sales	Total sales	NPV
Now	5	Nil	5	3
Option 1	4	Nil	4	2
Option 2	3.3	0.9	4.2	2.5
Option 3	2.9	1.6	4.5	2.3

(amounts in $ million)

drinkers. To meet this threat to its leading position the managers of Merry considered three options:

1. to do nothing;
2. to obtain Merry's own licence and to market its own alcotrop under the brand of Merritrop; and
3. to pursue option 2, but under the existing brand of Merry.

Option 3 would save the investment in a new brand, but would also dilute the traditional image of the Merry brand of lager, and lose some lager sales the following year which would be retained under option 2. The estimated effects of the three options are shown in Table 2.1.

Merry's best option is option 2, which yields the best NPV, not option 3 which maximizes sales. Merry should of course accept that neither total sales nor NPV might be maintained at the 'now' level enjoyed before Tipsy's move.

Financial Value: Valuation Criteria

Our valuation of a project should aim to apply the criteria which the stockmarket would apply to it, if it had our internal information about its prospects. The cost of capital should be taken as the rate the market applies now to any project with a similar risk profile and with the same time-frame. The time-frame depends on the payback period of the project. A new automobile model might have a payback period of 10 years from the decision to invest; a decision by a shop to invest in a fax service for customers might pay back in a matter of months. Merry's option 2 might have a payback period of 3 years.

The market's discount rate, like the price earnings ratio, is often volatile. The peaks and troughs of the market tend to overshoot, as for example at the end of the 1990s with the 'dotcom' boom. This is due to bandwagon effects caused by market participants watching each other rather than the underlying supply and demand. At times like that it may be advisable to make some normalizing adjustment to the current discount rate by consulting economists, or by reading experienced economic commentators in the press. During such exaggerated peaks and troughs economists tend to be surprisingly unanimous! The adjustment will necessarily be a guesstimate, but better than no adjustment. The discount rate has a powerful effect on the evaluation of any project, and its selection needs all the care we can give it.

Some important features of this NPV test are sometimes overlooked:

- The cash flows consist of *expectations*.
- The cash flows are incremental: they are the difference between the expected future cash flows of the company (a) with, and (b) without the offering. In the Merry example, option 1 is the reference point.
- The comparison is between cash flows, which exclude, for example, allocated costs or depreciation charged in the accounts.
- The cash flows must take into account any favourable or unfavourable effects on other parts of the company. For example, a new Starbuck outlet may not only take business away from other local coffee outlets, but also from the nearest Starbuck only a few streets away. Microsoft Windows 2020 may take business away from Windows 2018. In our alcotrop example the most important item is the effect of each option on sales of Merry lager.
- The discount rate varies with the risk of each individual new offering. An important element of that risk is that customers may prefer competing substitutes, some of them not yet on the market and thus unknown at the time of evaluation. What is the risk for Merry of liquor stores importing drinks from Australia?
- The test will have different results at different stages in the life of an offering. Expectations of future cash flows will change with fresh news, and so may the discount rate with reassessments of the risk factor.
- At the original evaluation of any option such as option 2 in the alcotrop case, any negative NPV would mean that the company

would be better off without that option, quite apart from the comparison with the alternatives.

- As the new offering goes through its lifespan, a time will inevitably come when the test will show the cumulative total value generated to date no longer growing, but declining. The offering has completed its useful life, and should *at that point* be discontinued or *divested*, as it has now begun to destroy value. See Figure 2.1 below.

The Value-Building Biography of an Offering

Figure 2.1 shows how an offering, like any investment project, will at first generate negative value during the cash-negative investment phase, and then build value as receipts from customers exceed payments. Then, if it is successful, it will build value until the cumulative value-to-date turns positive. That point is the end of the payback period. Hopefully, it will continue to build value after that until its competitive success is exhausted. There will come a point where it ceases to

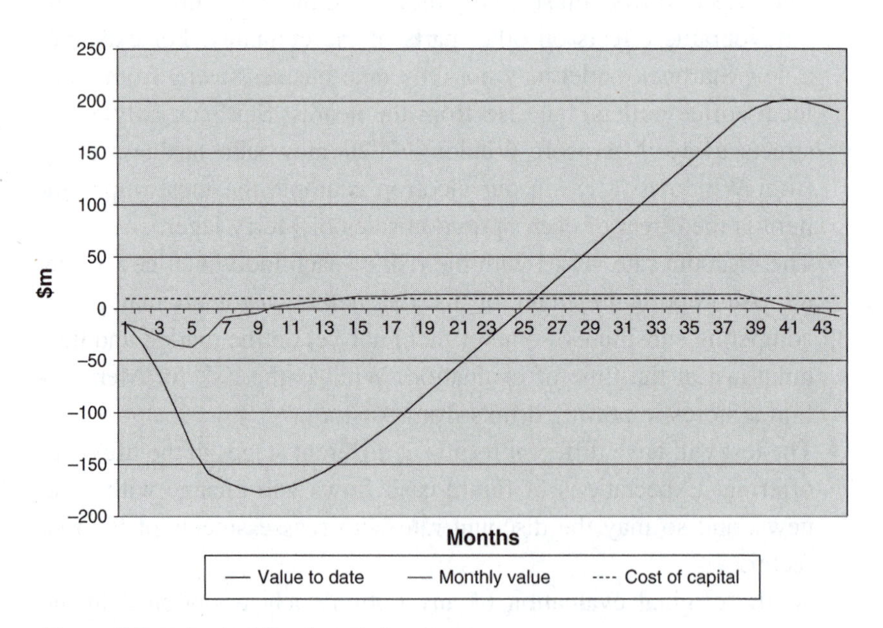

Figure 2.1 Value building by offering

build value and the cumulative value-to-date reaches its peak before declining. That peak point is when the offering should be divested, as it will after that destroy rather than generate value.

In Figure 2.1, monthly value is monthly cash, that is receipts less payments, less a notional interest charge representing the cost of capital. The value-to-date line is the cumulative version of monthly value.

The cost of capital is here represented by a monthly dollar charge which the monthly cash must beat if it is to build value. The cost of capital is in this context a notional dollar charge, not a discount factor, because in this context we are not seeking to calculate the net *present* value of the offering.

Value Generated in Commercial Markets

It is in their *commercial* markets that most businesses aim to generate value. They market offerings which outperform their competing substitutes enough to beat their cost of capital. The purpose of this book therefore is to describe the task of designing offerings which do that.

There is in fact another way of creating value, by pure dealing. Thus a trader in financial instruments like Soros, in metal or oils or other traded commodities, or even in corporate assets, such as KKR, creates value not from competing for customers, but by shrewdly buying cheap and selling dear in the markets concerned. Pure dealing is a different type of business, with which we are not concerned here.

The Company's Collection of Offerings

Merry is a company with two offerings. Most companies have more than one offering, and some large companies have thousands of offerings. Each offering has to be designed separately. Yet the company's collection of offerings also needs to be managed in its own right. In both cases the test is whether financial value is generated. The process of managing the collection we call corporate strategy. It constantly monitors the collection and makes decisions to add, retain or divest offerings. It will be described in Part 4.

A business like Merry comes into being if somebody invests in it, in the hope of earning a higher risk-adjusted return from Merry than from the next most attractive project Y. The return expected from Y is the opportunity cost of investing in Merry. The investor's opportunity cost is the expected return from Y which the investor forgoes by funding Merry.

A prominent task of corporate strategy is that of weeding out and divesting offerings which no longer add financial value to the company. This important task is described in Chapter 13.

The Value Objective and Its Stakeholder Rival: A Discussion

The first objection to the view a business exists to create financial value comes from those who regard it as morally and socially undesirable. The moral objection sees the financial view as a cold, ruthless and selfish attitude to human relations in business, opposed for example to the Christian imperatives of peace, love and compassion, which are to varying degrees shared by other religions, including Hinduism, and other ideologies. The closely related social objection sees the financial view as promoting narrow self-interest and conflict between competing class interests rather than the common good of society as a whole, which includes the ecology.

We hope to show that these objections rest on a misunderstanding of the nature and purpose of 'the business' or the company. We authors of this book certainly share the warmer and socially cohesive value systems of the objectors, but regard such value systems as perfectly compatible with the financial view, as that view should be understood. In any case, in a perfect world with well-functioning markets a company that creates long-term financial value by that very fact contributes to social well-being.[3]

The objectors support the opposing *stakeholder* view. This holds that business has a social purpose, and needs to serve the interests of other stakeholders as well as those of investors. Other stakeholders are usually listed as the environment, society at large, suppliers, customers and employees.

Conflict of loyalties?

Before discussing the merits of the stakeholder view, we hope to clarify one version of it, which has clouded the issue for many commentators. The stakeholder view is often presented as resolving a conflict of loyalties for managers. Do they owe loyalty just to the investors *as a group of people*, or to all the stakeholder groups?

Those who ask that question apply a mental model in which the manager sees her task as requiring loyalty to one or another group of human beings. The company is not a human being, hence cannot be an object of loyalty in that model. Loyalty is therefore seen as needing to be either to the investors who own the company or to all its stakeholder groups.

What conflicts in fact face real managers?

To deal with this loyalty issue, we need to set out first what in our own experience are the actual conflicts that face real managers. All these conflicts have two features in common. First, they are all between a manager's personal interests and the value objective of the company. Secondly, some ambivalence is here caused by the company's two very different roles, which each serve the interests of a defined group of people

1. as servant of its investors; and
2. as the employer, to whom the manager owes a contractual and professional duty.

In other words, managers' real conflicts are not between loyalties to different groups of people, such as stakeholders, but between their own and their colleagues' personal interests and those of the company they serve.

Managers are of course ethical human agents, and have their own value systems and consciences, but these are a part of each manager's personal interests, which may also point to conflicting courses of action. More about managers' personal value systems and interests later.

Yet when discussing managers' real conflicts, we need to separate out two sub-categories. Are we discussing conflicts

1. facing CEOs or all managers?
2. at times of a survival crisis or in calmer times?

The CEOs in relatively calm times face a conflict of interest mainly between investing in risky projects of high financial value, or safer ones of lower value. Riskier projects meet CEOs' duty to their employing companies; safer ones appear to be better for their own job security. Again, CEOs may be tempted to abuse their position of power to obtain pay, employment conditions and fringe benefits in excess of their market value to the company.

In a survival crisis CEOs might be tempted to take damaging steps designed either to bring about short-term improvements in the company's share price or to frustrate hostile bidders, for example by poison pills. Their own consciences usually prevail against these temptations. In any case financial market regulations and legal requirements have in many countries been tightened to prevent such actions and to safeguard the interests of investors.

All managers (including CEOs) may in calmer times be tempted to act to the detriment of the company's financial value by claiming reimbursement of unnecessary expenses, by personally consuming the company's property, or by obtaining other personal benefits at the company's expense.

Priorities tend to change in a survival crisis. In such a crisis all managers have a natural tendency to become preoccupied with their own and their closer colleagues' and their dependants' future, and to give more priority to these personal interests than to those of the company and its investors. This temptation is reinforced by the fact that at such times investors are apt to become less committed to the retention of the present management team.

If these reflections are correct, then the conflicts of interest are between manager Ann's own contractual and professional duty and her personal interests, which include her own and her closer colleagues' jobs and livelihood. This dilemma is not of course clear-cut between good and bad, between selfishness and conscience. In a survival crisis, if Ann chooses the path of duty, that will improve her chances of finding managerial employment elsewhere. If she chooses the other path, she may be motivated by compassion for close colleagues and their families, should they all lose their jobs.

What concerns us here is that Ann is not likely to be choosing between different groups of stakeholders. Ann will not think of the investors as people, if her public company has thousands of shareholders. To her these are a remote, faceless and constantly changing group of people. Her duty she sees as being not to them, but to her own integrity in a position of trust.

The survival crisis is a very common experience in modern times. It forces Ann into some agonizing decisions. In an extreme case her duty to the company and its investors is to recommend a hostile takeover bid, if it represents better value than whatever NPV the present management team's realistic plans provide. However, that recommendation may well lead to her own and her colleagues' redundancy, and to severe hardship for their families and dependants. The existing management team may well be close friends and deeply committed to each other's vital interests. The dilemma is moral, and very real. Much more real than any assumed choice between loyalty to investors and loyalty to all stakeholders.

In discussing the value objective, we have treated the investors as an abstraction, representing the financial interest in the company. Stakeholder theorists tend to treat them as real people, to whom managers feel some personal loyalty. That model may well fit the case where one or a few people or a family own the business, but hire others to manage. Ann, who is such an employee manager, may well face a dilemma if she thinks her owners are treating a supplier or a fellow employee harshly. That is because the owners are known to her personally.

However, stakeholder theorists mainly appear to have in mind the public company with thousands of shareholders. To Ann they are a faceless and constantly changing group of people. The idea that they command her *personal* loyalty may be a little far-fetched.

Which of the two views is more desirable?

Investors are interested in financial value, the other stakeholder groups have different and often mutually conflicting priorities. For example, the interests of trade unions are often opposed to those of customers. Hence the stakeholder view requires managers to hold some balance between those conflicting views. Investors want profits and dividends, employees want good pay, good working conditions and job security. Customers want low prices and efficient performance. All these conflicts can raise costs and reduce profit. Similarly, the interests of customers and suppliers and of the environment often reduce profit by raising costs or reducing selling prices.

Of course, looking after the interests of these other stakeholders also has some benign effects on profits. It avoids the costs of conflict, of pressures and of friction. British Airways' profits, for example, have been slashed more than once by damaging strikes. A company which cultivates the goodwill of its non-financial stakeholders and of their champions can operate more efficiently and smoothly. This is good for value creation. There is thus some built-in overlap between the interests of all the various stakeholders. The conflict is not head-on.

We believe the stakeholder view has one fatal drawback. Competitive business is a hard challenge. It needs to be directed by people who understand the parts played by all links in the value chain, to weld all parts of the effort together for single-minded thrust in the tough arena of competition. Management needs to be single-minded, and should not have to serve conflicting interests.[4] Financial value provides a single criterion of success. If managers are not focused on it, they are bound to fail. *The Economist* in a survey by Clive Crook puts it as follows:[5] 'Managers . . . ought not to concern themselves with the public good: they are not competent to do it, they lack the democratic credentials for it, and their day jobs should leave them no time even to think about it.'

The task of restricting the freedom of businesses to act against the public good is that of governments. Managers are the agents of the owners and must discharge their duty to them by serving the company's goal of financial value within the constraints imposed by governments and the law.

We asked which view is more desirable. Both have desirable features, and managers should not neglect those interests of non-financial stakeholders which promote the company's financial aims, such as good relations with employees. However, where the two views clash, the financial interest must in our view prevail.

Is the stakeholder view valid?

The stakeholder view may not be desirable as a statement of ultimate priority. However, is it valid? Does it fit the facts of competitive business?

The stakeholder view often sees the business or company as a collection of *human beings*, consisting of groups with various potentially conflicting interests. This is a *social* model. The financial view on the other hand sees the company as an inanimate object, as one or more investment projects. The business is 'born' as a vehicle to generate financial value – returns in excess of the cost of capital. It 'dies' when investors believe it is no longer capable of earning those returns. At that point the investors will either sell it, perhaps by accepting a takeover bid, or break it up to turn the assets into cash. In either case the managers will lose their power to look after the interests of employees or of any other stakeholders. This inanimate model of the company is a *financial* one.

The weakness of the social model is that it thinks of the company as a continuing and even immortal and permanent entity. It neglects its birth and death. Birth and death are the stages which disclose the true nature of the business. Companies are far from immortal. As competition intensified in the second half of the twentieth century, they were seen to be only too mortal. The inanimate model fits the facts, the social one does not. The stakeholder view is not just less desirable. It also represents a false model.

Short-term vs. long-term objectives

The survival crisis raises another big issue. Are investors interested in short- or long-term returns? It is not a matter of short or long, but of how long. Investors apply a discount factor to different future periods. Their concern is the NPV of expected future cash flows, discounted at the appropriate rate. Cash flows in distant periods are less valuable than imminent ones. What happens in the survival crisis is that the more distant periods attract a much higher risk factor and therefore lose even more of their attraction. This is equally true for investors and managers, both become preoccupied with the present.

There is nevertheless in the survival crisis also a conflict between the interests of managers and investors. Managers are bound to be concerned to preserve their and their colleagues' jobs; investors are only concerned with financial value.

Are we then left with the law of the jungle?

Our conclusion that the stakeholder view is neither tenable nor desirable is not widely shared. It seems to argue for an uncaring world of business in which the weak are left unprotected against brutal exploitation by the strong, in which managers are encouraged to be ruthless in satisfying greedy investors, and in which business is free to destroy the planet. We saw earlier that this is why so many object to the creation of value as the overriding purpose of business.

In this book we are certainly not arguing for such an uncaring view.[6] If the business exists to make money, the law of the jungle is nevertheless fought by a formidable array of counterforces:

1. As we have seen, the business itself has a *financial* interest in keeping the non-financial stakeholders happy enough to refrain from inflicting costs on companies.
2. Individual managers are human beings with moral values and consciences. In their business jobs they do not cease to be moral human beings, although in many situations they are aware that their softer inclinations conflict with the aims of the business. Managers are exposed to many tensions, and this is one of them. Many a manager has either become a whistleblower or resigned on grounds of conscience.
3. Collectively, teams of managers often have value systems which go beyond the financial goal and give a company a distinctive culture. John Kay has drawn attention to this.[7] He argues that this makes the company itself a moral agent. However, a company is not identical with its managing team. It can maintain its continuity despite a radical change of culture, as did GEC in Britain when in the late 1950s, Arnold Weinstock became its managing director. Again, such a softer collective culture of the management team can conflict with the overriding goal of the company. Nevertheless, it is a counterforce.
4. Society through the state imposes constraints on businesses to protect the weak, the environment and other features of the common good. It does this by means of a number of different mechanisms: laws, regulations and fiscal measures.
5. Society also makes its influence felt through pressure groups such as Amnesty International, non-governmental organizations like Cafod, Oxfam or Friends of the Earth, or purely local or special action groups and lobbies.

The role of the state is particularly important for two reasons inherent in the nature of some or all competitive markets:

1. Laws and regulations are needed to ensure that the costs of constraints hit all competing businesses equally. Otherwise each

competitor has a strong incentive to evade the constraint in order to obtain a cost advantage over its rivals.

2. In some markets the state alone can provide effective safeguards against domination by over-powerful market participants (Chapter 7). The state can impose anti-monopoly laws and regulations.

Businesses may exist to make money, but they operate in a social context. There is therefore plenty of scope for managers as human beings to act ethically and in a socially responsible way. In formulating an ethical framework for themselves, managers may well find the stakeholder view helpful. It lists and describes the interests to which managers may wish to pay attention, individually or collectively. On the other hand, we find no scope for treating the company or business as an ethical agent or as having an ethical purpose. There is therefore also no visible scope for *corporate* social responsibility in the sense that the company has it in its own right. It is a different matter if (say) its customers require it to *act* with social responsibility. The company does exist to win and serve profitable customers, and they can impose corporate social responsibility on the company by proxy.

In a nutshell, the company's purpose is to optimize its value in its various financial, commercial, labour and other markets. However, markets themselves are not shaped just by raw nature. If they were, all business might be conducted on Mafia lines! Markets work on natural human motives like self-interest, but are heavily influenced by society, through laws, regulations, public opinion, actions of pressure groups and religious bodies.

In any case, companies are managed by people, and people are moral agents, who may in conscience be unable to accept pure market motives even with all the social constraints imposed on those markets. If managers act in accordance with their consciences and reject the logic of markets, they need to be aware of the fact that they are in conflict with the purpose of the company. In a survival scenario that conflict could jeopardize the company's independent survival. The distinction between the aims of the inanimate business and those of the individuals managing it is therefore not trivial. It needs to be made. We may deplore conflict, but we cannot wish it away.

The Objective of Risk Diversification

We now turn to the two *internal* objectives that conflict with that of financial value. In the second half of the twentieth century two false gods were in vogue among managers, risk diversification and size. The less influential of these was risk diversification. The idea was to make the company safer by diluting its risk profile. A caricature of this would be a civil contractor acquiring a dealer in bankrupt stocks. Contracting is a highly cyclical business, vulnerable to recessions, whereas dealing in bankrupt stocks is countercyclical; it thrives in a recession. The same logic might prompt a silicon chips maker to add potato chips to its collection. A classic example was BAT Industries in the mid-twentieth century. To diversify its exposure to the risks of anti-smoking regulation or consumers shifting away from cigarettes, BAT acquired a number of companies, among them a cosmetics producer and Eagle Star, an insurance company. The acquisitions were unsuccessful for many reasons.

The theoretical case for risk diversification was in any case undermined by the recognition that the risks could be more cheaply diversified by investors in their portfolios than physically by the companies in which they invested. In short, if the intention of risk diversification was to make the companies more valuable to investors, that purpose fell flat on its face. It made them less attractive to investors.

The Objective of Size

The more influential false god, however, was size. The unquestioned belief was that companies should aim to become bigger. Bigger in what sense? Size was thought of in a number of ways, including number of management units, physical size of real estate or plants, volume of sales, number of employees, financial size or market capitalization (number of shares issued multiplied by share price), economies of scale, market power or dominance in either buying or customer markets.

The last two objectives, scale economies and market power in either buying or selling, can of course be genuine sources of financial value. They can give a company better margins in its markets. Whether they will in any given case have that effect depends, however, on other factors like the reactions of customers and competitors. By themselves they do not guarantee success. Will customers, for example, resent a supplier's takeover of a competitor and show their resentment by defecting to a smaller independent firm or lobbying for anti-monopoly intervention by the authorities? Customers do not like having their choice restricted.

These two apart, the listed items have no inherent power to boost long-term financial performance. Raising turnover will not raise earnings if the extra sales are loss making. New shares issued for a bad acquisition will reduce earnings per share. Extra physical capacity may raise or reduce unit costs. So may the occupation of extra space. The track record suggests that on balance growth in sheer size reduces rather than adds value.

Why Has the God of Size Been so Influential?

The drive for size was universal doctrine for much of the twentieth century. Moreover, many managers are still pursuing it in the twenty-first century; long after it lost its respectability. Why has it been so powerful for so long?

One reason has been the widespread belief that financial size, meaning market capitalization, protects against hostile takeover. Note that bid-proofing the company is attractive to managers, as opposed to investors.

That widespread belief is not wholly without foundation. A $100 company is an unlikely bidder for Microsoft. What does not follow, however, is that an increase in financial size *without a rise in financial value* – that is in the value of a given investor's holding – will of itself reduce vulnerability to takeover. As we have just noted, new shares issued for a bad acquisition will reduce earnings per share and thus value.

In fact we may destroy financial value to the point where even our market capitalization is less than before the new share issue. Our share price was £2.00, and we had an issued capital of 1 million shares. Our market capitalization was thus £2 000 000. We now make a rights issue of one for four shares @ £1.60 in order to acquire Disaster Inc. The issue of another 250 000 shares brought in £400 000 cash. However,

Disaster's losses made our share price fall from the issue price of £1.60 to £1.20. We now had 1 250 000 shares capitalized by the market at £1 500 000. This was a 25 per cent drop from £2 000 000 before the deal, despite the inflow of £400 000 cash from the share issue! The attempt to boost size had been self-defeating.

Now suppose the share price had risen from the issue price of £1.60 to £1.80 instead of falling to £1.20. Market capitalization would then have risen to £2 250 000, an increase of £250 000 from the original £2 million. Would that have increased financial value? No, because the increase is less than the £400 000 cash raised. The holder of 100 shares, originally worth £200, would have paid out £40 for an extra 25 shares. His 125 shares would now have a market value @ £1.80 of £225, a loss of £15 from the £200 + £40 (original value plus cash subscribed), total £240. The company would have become more, not less vulnerable to takeover. The shareholders now have reason to welcome any bidder who might offer them more than a mere £1.80 per share. Market capitalization is not the figure we need to boost if we wish to remain independent. What managers must boost is their financial performance, so as to leave no room for others to improve on it.

An even worse reason for the drive for size is the aim of some unscrupulous top managers to boost their own status and remuneration by boosting the size of the company they are running. A well-designed service contract harmonises the personal interests of top managers with those of the investors in the company. However, managers should not be rewarded for boosting size without boosting financial value. In all such cases managers are acting against the interests of the company. This is a conflict of interest. To feather one's own nest at the expense of the prosperity of one's company breaches a contractual as well as a moral duty. Since Enron, WorldCom, Parmalat and other scandals such conduct is increasingly penalized by corporate law and financial market regulations.

A very different matter is the case where the motive is to boost financial value rather than personal status. Size *can* go hand in hand with financial value, even though that is less common than many people believe.

There are also some popular fallacies that encourage the pursuit of size in the sense of market share or market domination. John Kay wrote an article about this.[8] He had found that managers in pharmaceuticals, defence contracting, in utilities and advertising, in banks and law firms expected their 'industries' to become ever more globally concentrated, with only a few survivors in each case. They all apparently saw the car industry as the example that would inevitably be followed by their own industries. This belief clearly encouraged them to go for market share in widely defined global markets. Kay points out that this belief misreads the history of the car industry. Its peak of concentration had in fact occurred in the early 1950s. In the late 1960s the big three (General Motors, Ford and Chrysler) made half the world's cars. In 2003, the then big three (General Motors, Ford and Toyota) only made 36 per cent of world output. Small carmakers had been steadily gaining market share at the expense of large ones. As real unit costs and prices had declined, so had the importance of price and economies of scale. More affluent customers were less and less influenced by price. Their tastes became less uniform. The former mass market moved towards a series of niche markets in which different customers preferred different models from different car-makers. Share of the wider car market was no longer what mattered.

We conclude that the only way to ensure the independent survival of a business is by generating financial value. Size by itself will not do the trick, nor will risk diversification, nor will a stakeholder objective.

Illustration: Lloyds Bank Under Sir Brian Pitman

In a striking article in *Harvard Business Review*, Sir Brian Pitman, CEO of Lloyds Bank 1983–2001, makes just these points.[9] During his period of office the growth of shareholder value averaged 26 per cent a year. During that same period Midland Bank and National Westminster Bank lost their independence.

Sir Brian wanted

> a single, well-defined performance measurement, one that would replace our existing array of implicit objectives: Serve shareholders, serve customers, serve employees, serve society in general. Such woolly goals

> get you nowhere because they aren't specific enough to have an effect on people's performance.... Without this focus, I feared we would muddle along, our efforts diluted by the pursuit of multiple goals.

The Lloyds Bank board decided to go for return on equity, and after flirting with an objective of a return of 10 per cent, which was above the prevailing rate of inflation of 5 per cent, they realized that the proper goal was to beat the cost of equity. They then had a shock when they found that the cost of equity was between 17 and 19 per cent.

> we undertook a major analysis . . . to determine which of our businesses were creating value and which were destroying it. We found that a small proportion of the company's operations were generating most of the value, while more than half of them were earning less than the cost of capital and thus dragging our share price down. This analysis led us to exit markets like California, which we calculated, contributed an 8% return on equity at a time when our cost of equity was more than double that.

In the mature market of commercial banking Sir Brian's achievement was astonishing. Like this book, he assigned a key role to the objective of beating the cost of capital.

Lloyds Bank subsequently ran into difficulties after acquiring Scottish Widows, but that does not diminish this achievement and the wisdom of the corporate objective behind it.

Summary and Conclusion

We can sum this important chapter up as follows:

- Financial value is in fact the criterion by which companies succeed or fail, survive or go under. That is easily demonstrated from any glance at past business failures and disasters.
- We need an objective which stands the test of time: other goals have been tried not just in Marxist societies, but also in countries like Japan, and found wanting.
- We also need a single-minded objective. Managing for success is not easy. It becomes downright impossible if managers pursue more than one, let alone conflicting goals.

Notes

1. See any reputable text on finance, for example Brealey, R.A. and Myers, S.C. (2000). *Principles of Corporate Finance*. Sixth edition. New York: McGraw-Hill.
2. For a fuller discussion of the shortcomings of accounting numbers, see Rappoport, A. (1986). *Creating Shareholder Value: The New Standard for Business Performance*. New York: Free Press. See also, Stewart, G.B. (1991). *The Quest for Value*. New York: Harper Business.
3. Jensen, M.C. (2001). Value maximization, stakeholder theory, and the corporate objective function. *Journal of Applied Corporate Finance*, Fall, **14**(3), 8–21.
4. For a persuasive discussion, see Ibid.
5. Crook, C. (2005). The good company: a survey of corporate social responsibility. *The Economist*, 22 January 2005, p. 18.
6. See also, Sternberg, E. (1995). *Just Business*. London: Warner Books.
7. Kay, J. (2004). Corporate character is not just a legal construct. *Financial Times*, 7 December 2004, p. 23.
8. Kay, J. (2003). Survival of the fittest, not the fattest. *Financial Times*, 27 March 2003, p. 21.
9. Pitman, B. (2003). Leading for value. *Harvard Business Review*, April.

3

The basics of designing a winning offering

Introduction

We saw in Chapters 1 and 2 that the new offering we are designing must build value by beating the cost of capital, and that for this it needs a winning competitive position and one or more winning resources. In a word, the offering must *excel in a target arena.*

This chapter sets out in general terms the key conditions that make an offering a winner, the threats that the offering has to overcome, why both a winning competitive position and winning resources are needed to overcome those threats, and the yardsticks of success at various stages. Parts 2 and 3 discuss these issues in greater detail.

The Offering and Its Competitive Position

An offering is what customers can choose. Customers choose not in a vacuum, but by considering their other options, such as competing substitutes. An offering is therefore defined by how customers see it in relation to rival offerings. That triangular relationship between the offering and its potential substitutes in the eyes of choosing customers is its competitive position. Its competitive position is unique to each offering and identifies it. They are in a one-for-one relationship, like the two sides of the same coin. If exactly the same model of a popular car has a different competitive position in country A than in country B because it faces different rival offerings or different customer preferences, then it is two distinct offerings, one in each country and requires two distinct competitive strategies. Figures 3.1 and 3.2 illustrate this for a personal computer (PC).

Similarly, what may superficially look like a number of offerings may in fact be a single one. A supermarket sells thousands of goods, but customers choose one of several competing supermarkets for their weekly shopping. Each of them is a single competing offering, with a price consisting of its weighted average price or mark-up compared with the corresponding weighted average figure of its rivals. British customers overwhelmingly do not buy their apples from one supermarket and their tea from another. The competition is not between the apples or the teas they each sell, but between the total shopping experiences offered by each competing supermarket.

The triangular relationship hinges on customers' *perceptions*. If toy engine A is made of stainless steel and engine B of plastic, and if B is preferred by customers at the same price, then B is the superior offering for this purpose.

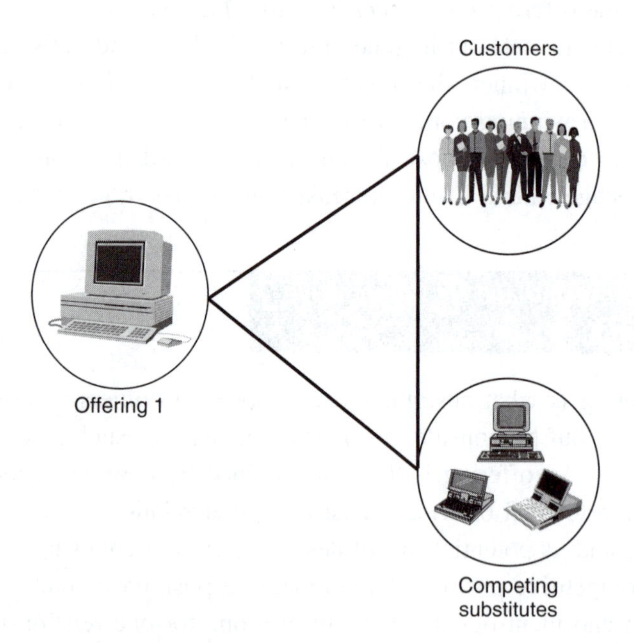

Figure 3.1 Original triangular relationship

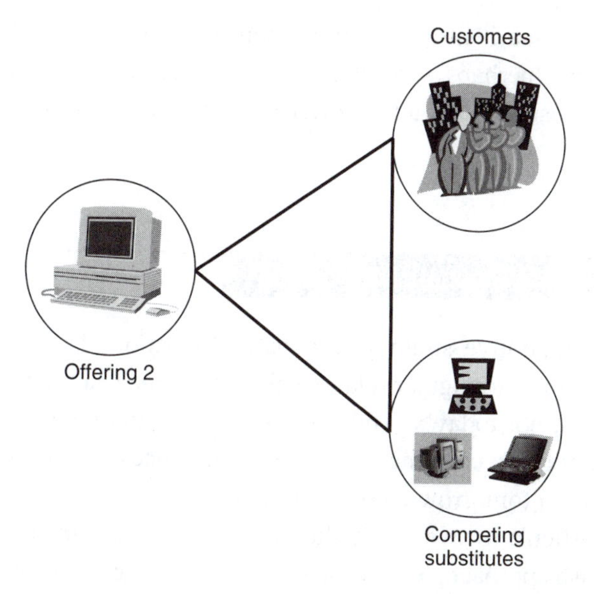

Figure 3.2 New triangular relationship: changed customers and substitutes

Competitive Positions Are Not Immortal

Because each offering is identified by its competitive position, offerings frequently have a shorter life than is widely believed. Competitive positions have a way of shifting. We ourselves may upgrade or reposition our offering, a competitor may modify its rival offering, or finally customers themselves may shift their preferences. In the latter case they may, for example, find mink coats no longer ethically acceptable, or they may come to regard London tube travel as unsafe. In any such case, whether it is we ourselves, or a competitor, or the customers who have shifted, our offering now finds itself in a new triangular position vis-à-vis customers and competitors. Customers now face a different pattern of choices much like the buyers of the same model of the popular car in countries A and B. The changed competitive position has made it a new offering: even if it retains such a great deal of continuity that it obviously belongs to the same genre. For example, our generic offering's market share may have changed up or down.

The creation of a new offering may therefore be quite undramatic and relatively unnoticed, but the event is no less important for that.

If customers see it in a new light, then the value of the offering has changed too, perhaps substantially. The seller needs to review and perhaps reposition it as a *new* offering: that is the task of competitive strategy.

Tomorrow's Competitive Position

What a competitive strategy designs and positions is a future offering: *tomorrow's* triangular relationship with *tomorrow's* customers and competitors, not today's. Today's competitors and their present positions, and today's customers and their preferences, are of interest only as pointers to tomorrow's configuration.

It is difficult to overstress this point. Too many managers take a broad-brush approach. Surely the radical upgrading of my own offering will automatically ensure that tomorrow's customers see it as repositioned? No, not automatically. Not if all competitors are seen to make identical improvements. If they do, then there is no change in my or their competitive positioning. If we were all the same today, we will all be the same tomorrow. The only correct benchmark for competitive strategy is rival offerings tomorrow, not our offering today.

The task of developing a competitive strategy must therefore include a searching analysis of competitors. The task is:

- to identify future competing substitutes;
- to do this for each of our offerings, not collectively for all offerings; and
- to identify future rival offerings by researching the old and new firms likely to offer them.

Threats to a Competitive Position

A proposed new offering can be a winner only if it can be expected to produce the required positive cash flows for the entire payback period. If it is to succeed, it must overcome various threats, and in order to overcome those threats it needs protective armour.

Threats can take many forms. The main ones are these:

a. offerings have a limited commercial life; customers will find other things to spend their money on, or the offerings become technically obsolete, or more attractive substitutes come into the market;
b. when an offering is seen to earn high returns, it attracts imitators; competitors move in, prices and margins get eroded.

These threats can be on either the demand or the supply side. The demand side includes the case where customers' preferences move away. The supply side includes shortages or cost increases affecting supplies or labour. Our own protective armour against those threats can also be on either side. On the demand side, market barriers may protect our competitive position against encroachment by competitors. On the supply side, we need our very own winning resources to attract and retain customers and keep competitors at bay. Those resources are the subject of Part 3.

Protective armour

There are three kinds of protective armour. All three are barriers against unrestricted competition:

1. Market barriers: these restrict entry into this market. Market barriers are described in Chapter 7. They include regulations or laws restricting entry, or cultural resistance by buyers against new entrants, and the like.
2. Differentiation (Chapters 4–6): our offering has features which customers find preferable to those of its substitutes, and which competitors cannot easily copy.
3. Entry barriers on the supply side, such as steep capital costs of entry, or more generally lower unit costs which cannot easily be replicated or bettered by competitors.

Whether the offering will actually be a winner depends on both demand and supply side factors.[1] It needs a potentially winning competitive position and also winning resources. The competitive position must be sufficiently durable to make it a potential winner. For example, we need solid grounds for believing that competitors cannot or will not during that period launch superior offerings, or erode our returns by price reductions. Equally, we must be confident, for example, that the preferences of customers will not autonomously move away from our proposed new offering during the payback period through changes in tastes and fashions, or ethical values. Changes in preferences are for this purpose 'autonomous' if they are not prompted by our own or our competitors' actions. We must of course allow for some changes. Finally we need solid grounds for believing that the competitive position will not weaken so as to invalidate the assumptions made in our investment decision.

Are Winning Resources on Their Own Enough?

Part 3 examines the winning resources needed to protect the offering against adverse changes in its market. Are those resources by themselves enough to ensure a positive NPV? No. For example, what we have called autonomous threats to the competitive position can be outside the reach of those resources. That is why we must carefully analyse the competitive position and satisfy ourselves that risks of autonomous changes are small enough to justify a commitment to our planned offering and competitive position. We need protective armour against all market threats for the whole payback period.

The Yardstick at the Time of Planning a New Offering

We have said that to be a winner, the new offering must beat its cost of capital. But over exactly what period? The NPV, of the offering, discounted back to *the date of the decision* to create the offering, must be positive. In other words, the cumulative discounted value of the offering must become positive at a specific stage of its life. The period between the decision and the date when the value is expected to become positive is the payback period.

In Figure 2.1, we follow the value created by the offering each month. This cannot be done in terms of discounting back to the base date. So for practical purposes we use monthly cashflow debited with a notional monthly interest charge for the cost of capital. We here call the monthly result 'monthly value', and the cumulative value from the date of the investment decision 'value-to-date'.

In Chapter 2 we saw the value biography of a typical offering, and noted the precise meaning of beating the cost of capital. As Figure 2.1 shows, the value-to-date actually achieved by the offering is normally negative at first, due to the initial cash outflow when we invest in the offering. Only when the offering is later on launched and sold in the market, can it earn any returns. Moreover, the value built by initial sales often fails to clear the cost of capital. Only when volume has picked up will the returns exceed the cost of capital. That is when real value begins to be generated. The achieved negative value-to-date will then be whittled down until it turns positive. At that point the payback period ends.

The company will then of course aim to build more and more value, so that the achieved positive value grows. When the offering has become mature, returns often decline, but as long it still generates value, that is as long as the value-to-date still rises, the offering can continue trading. When it finally ceases to build value, it should be discontinued or sold. That point is covered more intensively in Part 4. If we allowed the achieved value-to-date of the offering to decline, we should be destroying value instead of creating it.

We said just now that the offering 'can' continue trading after the end of the payback period. It should of course do this if it is still building value, unless we choose to replace it with an upgrade or modification which will earn even better returns and perhaps enjoy a stronger position in the market. But that is an aside and conceptually no different from discontinuing one offering and introducing another.

Our present point is simply that when we design a new offering, we must at that time be satisfied that we can expect it to reach the end of the payback period, and to attain a positive value-to-date. That is the yardstick of success for the purpose of that investment decision.

We have had to describe this yardstick in terms of the value expected to be *achieved* cumulatively at the various future stages of its life by the offering. That is what the strategist has to consider when deciding whether to go ahead with a given proposed offering. Of course, the yardstick has important implications for the requirement in any given period during the life of the offering.

Yardsticks to be Applied After the Initial Decision

At subsequent stages yardsticks are needed (a) for monitoring implementation and (b) for retain/divest decisions.

For *monitoring* purposes the strict yardstick is the original projection. At any stage we can ask: by now we should show a value-to-date of –£25 000 in the start-up period, or perhaps +£10 000 a year after launch. How does the actual figure compare with that? However, after a year or so from the decision to invest in the offering, the cumulative figure will become less and less relevant. First, those responsible for implementation must increasingly focus on what is currently happening and remediable. Secondly, the original projection tends to become less and less relevant due to new factors that could not reasonably have been foreseen when the projections were made. The main question now is whether value is still being generated at a rate that justifies the effort put into the offering.

The monitoring yardstick thus moves at these later stages towards the yardstick for the retain/divest decision. That decision is no longer concerned with the recovery of the original cost of capital. *Decisions* must always deal with options for the future, not with the past.

The yardstick for *the retain/divest decision* is whether the offering can be expected to generate value *from now on*. If yes, we should retain it, if no, divest it. The principle is the same: the base date is that of the *decision*. Our judgement will of course owe much to the performance of the offering in the current period. If it is not building value, is this a temporary dip, with well-founded prospects of improvement? If it is currently building value, are there good grounds for believing that this will continue? The data on which we judge are at least in part backward-looking, but the judgement itself must look forward. In any case the decision may also need to take account of repercussions on other offerings.

Operating Conditions of Success

We have now settled the yardsticks of success. How does all this work out in operating terms? In operating terms the price of the offering must exceed its unit cost by more than the cost of capital. This is where the reactions and preferences of customers play an important part. There are many different prices that can be charged, but normally there will be a different volume of sales at each different price. There is the well-known trade-off between volume and margin. We must choose whatever price/volume combination gives us the best return not just in one period, but progressively over the payback period. If we price too low at the outset, there is a limit to the increases we can achieve later.

The unit margin that results must beat the cost of capital. That means that the customer as well as the company must derive value from the offering. Finally, value-generating margins must be sustained over the whole payback period. These operating conditions of success are well-known to all managers. The focus here is on the expectations at the time of the decision to invest in the new offering, and on the need for those expectations to be robust. We shall return to that last need a number of times, especially in Chapter 13.

Summary

This chapter has described the basics of designing a winning offering. It has set out the main issues of a winning competitive position and winning resources and their sustainability for at least the whole of the payback period. Winning competitive positions are covered in Part 2. Winning resources are dealt within Part 3. It has also set out the yardsticks of success, just what it means for the offering to beat its cost of capital. The practical process which achieves all this, which we call the scissors process, is the subject of Chapter 10.

Note

1. Priem, R.L. and Butler, J.E. (2001). Is the resource-based 'view' a useful perspective for strategic management research? *Academy of Management Review*, **26**(1), 22–40.

PART 2

How to Design a Winning Competitive Position

Part 2 deals with a central issue of competitive strategy: the key task of designing a winning competitive position. In other words, with the first of the two conditions of success. Chapters 4–7 therefore look at the external conditions, which need to apply in the market where customers will buy our offering. Part 3 will set out the second condition, that is the internal requirements that make an offering a winning one: the need for the offering to exploit one or more of the company's own winning resources.

As explained in Chapter 1, it is a key feature of our message that both these sets of requirements must be met to make the offering a winning one. Only then can it be expected to generate financial value.

4

Why and how to differentiate

This chapter introduces and describes differentiation, which is a key issue of competitive positioning and strategy.

Inputs and Outputs

The triangular relationship between an offering and its competing substitutes in the eyes of customers is its competitive position. That was illustrated in Figures 3.1 and 3.2. Offerings are competitively positioned in terms of differentiation and price. An offering is differentiated when it is seen by customers to be different and preferable to its competing substitutes in any way other than in price. Differentiation like competing prices has an effect on customers' choices.

An understanding of this important point is greatly helped by the distinction between inputs and outputs. Both are elements of an offering. Outputs are those elements which influence customers' choices. Inputs play a role in making and shaping the offering, but not in those choices. So the distinction turns on whether customers' choices are affected.

The exceptional picture quality of a television set is clearly an output, but the technical superiority of its circuit boards is unlikely to be an output: it constitutes an input, as in itself it does not normally influence the choosing customer. A trickier example is the production process of Krispy Kreme doughnuts.[1] They are usually produced in front of customers' eyes, in the belief that this will make them more attractive to customers. That effect on choosing customers makes the production process an output. The back office of a firm of accountants in itself usually has absolutely no effect on clients, in which case it is merely an input. However, it could in a special case affect a client's choice of firm and be an output. What matters is not of course some objective truth nor the intrinsic nature of a feature such as the back office, but whether customers are influenced by it. The back office that wins clients may in fact be less effective than its rivals. No, it is the *perceptions* of customers that matter here, and whether that back office affects those perceptions.

Penrose made a useful distinction when she wrote that '[s]trictly speaking, it is never *resources* themselves that are the "inputs" in the production process, but only the *services* that the resources can render'.[2] We only amplify that distinction when we suggest that strictly speaking characteristics such as components, production processes, back offices and so on are not inputs or outputs in themselves, but they have input and output effects. In principle any item, effort, resource or operation at any point along the entire value chain that generates an offering can have both these properties.

What matters here is that differentiation is a customer-centred concept. It needs to be described and measured in output, not input terms. We shall have more to say on this point in the next chapter.

What Exactly is Differentiation?

A strategy of differentiation is the design of a future offering which to some degree and in one or more dimensions – other than price – will be seen by potential customers as different, and preferable to its competing substitutes. The substitutes are of course tomorrow's substitutes for tomorrow's offering.

That statement is less simple than it may seem. Two toothpastes may be identical to an analysing chemist, but if choosing customers see valuable differences between them, for example between their brands, then they are differentiated. What sways choices is not some 'objective' truth, but the *perceptions* of customers. The efforts or resources, which the seller has put into them, matter only if they influence customers when they choose. In other words, they must either be outputs or produce outputs which are preferred by at least some customers.

Different from what? The comparison is always with the nearest competing substitutes. Differentiation is not achieved unless at least some customers prefer the offering to its substitutes which lack the differentiating feature, or rather would choose it if it were sold at the same price.

Merely being different from something else does not differentiate an offering. A printer, which includes a fax machine and a scanner, is 'different' from the stand-alone printer. However, if customers were to regard it as undistinguishable from other combined machines, then they would choose on price and treat this offering as undifferentiated.

Nor does differentiation simply mean high quality. If all the restaurants in our town had the same luxury standard of cuisine, with white tablecloths and napkins and waiters in smart uniforms and were all equally attractively located, they would all be undifferentiated. Choices would in that case be swayed just by price differences. Nor will a differentiated offering necessarily be bought by those who prefer it. Customers might be enticed away from it by a lower price. Differentiated is not the same thing as better value for money.

Positioning: Differentiation vs. Pure Competition

Offerings are positioned in customers' eyes in terms of differentiation and price. Where there is no differentiation, competition is just on price. Price is the only point of interest. Such a market is described in economics as that of *pure competition.*[3] Price will settle down at the lowest level offered by any of many competitors, and profitability will depend purely on unit costs. As long as there are significant fixed costs, profitability will partly depend on economies of scale, and therefore on market share. This suits the seller with the lowest unit costs, who must ultimately win that game.

Hundred per cent pure competition is rare in real life, but the concept is of practical use to managers. First, where differentiation is low, markets can still approximate to pure competition.

Secondly, the price-centred model of pure competition helps us to understand the effect and purpose of differentiation. Differentiation serves to switch customers' attention from price to the individual attractions of our particular offering. When the various toothpastes on offer vary in flavour, in the colour of the pack, in what customers believe is their effect on tooth decay, or in the reassurance offered by the reputation of the brand, then customers start choosing with an eye on the distinctive features of each competing offering, as well as price. They no longer choose just on price, but on value for money. How much more are customers willing to pay for their preferred Colgate-Palmolive toothpaste than for the less attractive Brand X offering? Will it take a 5, 10, 20 or 50 per cent lower price to make them buy Brand X? Competition is now between *offerings* and their different features, not just between their prices.

Why differentiate?

Before we describe *how* we can differentiate our offerings, we must be clear about *why* we do it. Differentiation does something for our customers, but what will it do for us? If we sell an undifferentiated offering, then we are inviting the customer to choose purely on price. The effect on us, on the seller is that differentiation makes our offering less price-sensitive. We no longer have to sell it at the price of the cheapest substitute. Our profits now depend less on volume. We have more latitude in our pricing policy. We can price higher for less sales at more margin, or lower for more market share at a smaller margin. We move some way at least from being mere price-takers to being price-setters. That option is an important benefit of differentiation. Most decisions about competitive positions are about how to differentiate.

Moreover, the *degree* of differentiation, which our toothpaste achieves, is not a matter of how much we add of some highly valued ingredient like fluoride, but of the percentage by which Brand X has to undercut us to keep its market share. That is what measures the degree of differentiation.

Figure 4.1 illustrates this. Our proposed offering is provisionally intended to sell at a price of 100. Substitute A would be preferred by a typical choosing customer if sold at 90, or at a discount of 10 per cent to ours. Substitute B would need a 20 per cent discount, and substitute C a 40 per cent discount. Our offering is most differentiated from C and least differentiated from A. That information can guide us in deciding whether to sell our offering against all substitutes at say 100, at 105, at 97 or any other price depending on what margin/volume combination builds the most value for us.

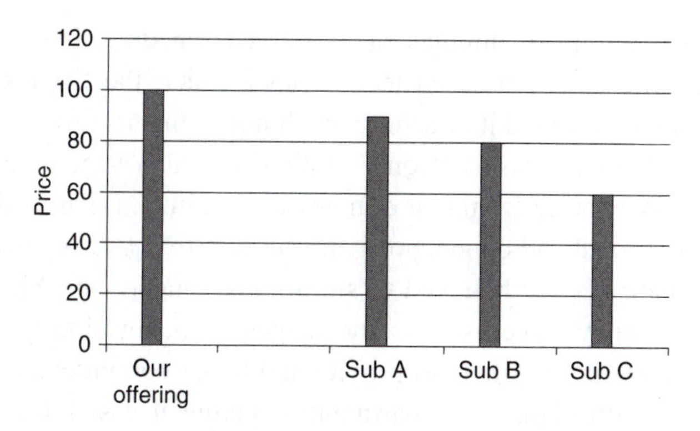

Figure 4.1 Price placing of competing offerings

How to differentiate

Figure 4.2 illustrates that an offering can be differentiated from its nearest substitutes

a. in various dimensions;
b. by various distances.

There need be no limit to the number of dimensions. The distance is also infinitely variable, as long as the offerings are still competing substitutes.

Virtually all offerings can be differentiated in one or another dimension. Cemex, the Mexican cement company, differentiated its offering not so much by the quality of its cement, but by the fact that in some congested urban areas it guaranteed delivery of ready-mix concrete

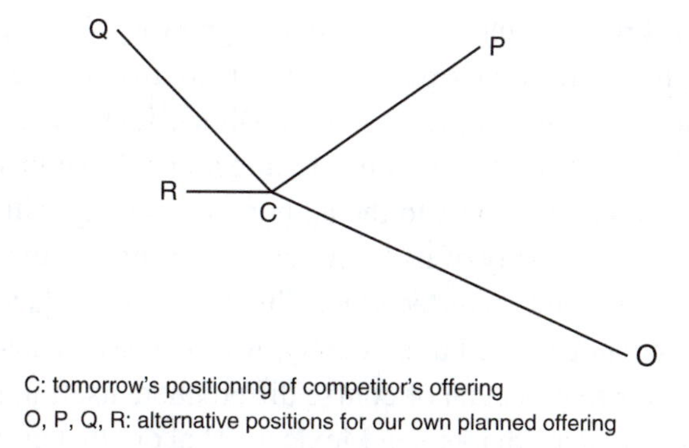

Figure 4.2 Qualitative and quantitative distancing of planned new offering

to builders within 20 minutes of an agreed schedule. It did this by using satellite and web-based technology.[4] Haier, the Chinese appliance maker, redesigned its washing machines so that its rural customers could use them to wash not only clothes, but also vegetables.[5] This distanced its offering from that of many competitors. BT is said to provide better broadband connections and support to domestic customers. Duracell batteries are believed to simply last longer. The Nationwide Building Society advertises its mortgages as being simply simpler. Dell was only recently held to provide not better computers, but better integration with client IT departments, making it easier for them to specify, order, obtain and maintain their PC systems.[6] Its closer relationship with customers would make it harder for those customers to switch to competitors.

A garage servicing cars can differentiate itself from its closest rival in many dimensions. The dimensions can include, for example:

- convenience of location;
- loan of a courtesy car during service or even collection of cars from owners and return after service;
- washing and valeting included as part of the service;
- friendliness of staff who are in contact with customers;
- ease of contact by telephone or other means;
- consultation with customer about faults found and cost of correction;
- degree of detail and clarity of itemized bill;
- quality of service, judged by results; and
- speed of service (e.g. through ready availability of parts).

Any one of these dimensions lends itself to infinite degrees of differentiation. For example, the location might vary from a congested cul-de-sac distant from any public transport to a very accessible location close to a subway or railway station. Dimensions can also differentiate competing substitutes in opposite directions. Customers compare a gourmet restaurant, known to the authors, favourably with its closest competitors in the quality of its food, service, decor, seating and tables, but not in its less attractive location. This drawback reduces the price differential it can charge, but evidently also reduces its space costs.

A gourmet restaurant can of course differentiate itself in many other ways. There are niche markets in Mexican, Thai or other ethnic cuisine, in vegetarian or fish dishes, in extras like cabaret, in dance floors, live music, privacy for courting couples and many other special features. All these are further instances of multidimensional segmentation, of addressing specialized smaller but high-margin markets. An offering need not outdo its competing substitutes in all dimensions in order to be differentiated. What counts is that target customers prefer it in the dimensions of interest to them.[7] A three-star suburban hotel next to a beautiful lake with wildfowl could be differentiated from its many identical, and thus undifferentiated, five-star urban rivals.

We return to the example of the service garage. All comparisons are with the nearest rivals to the service garage, nearest in the sense of being most likely to be chosen instead, not necessarily closest geographically. For example, the nearest rival may be a somewhat distant service centre for the same make of luxury car. The comparisons are *not* with some abstract concept of a basic or luxury service garage. Moreover, all the comparisons are in terms of outputs, in terms of how customers see the offering and its competing substitutes.

What about price competition?

The alternative to differentiation is to compete on price, but that ultimately tends to mean competing on costs, and especially unit costs where there are economies of scale. The less differentiation there is in a market, the keener will price competition be. All players in such a market will work hard to cut costs until they all settle at the lowest of tolerable margins over cost. When that happens, it is quite usual for the competitor with the highest market share to be the only one that earns its cost of capital. The others are under water. Winner takes all: hence Porter's doctrine that the alternative to differentiation is cost leadership.[8] Our company will be wise to compete on price alone only if it has the means of winning that cost and volume leadership and retaining it against the inevitable challenges that must follow.

A no-frills offering such as cheap air travel when first introduced by a European low-cost airline was not, as some may think, an attempt at 'negative differentiation'. First, the offering competes on price and thus not on differentiation and secondly, it is unlikely to remain unmatched if it thrives. Nimble potential rivals can restrain incumbents by the mere threat of competition. The market is said to be 'contestable' by them.[9] Therefore, it is best to regard such an offering as being essentially undifferentiated and relying on low costs for its continuing success.

Low unit costs depend on two factors. One is how the seller's costs compare with those of its competitors. The other is sales volume and market share. The first is therefore a matter of the resources discussed in Part 3, and the second a matter of competitive positioning which we examine in this Part 2.

In any event, the absence of differentiation also depends on whether customers have uniform preferences. This only occurs in pure or nearly pure commodity markets. A current UK example might be diesel fuel for motor vehicles. In the developed world, rising incomes have led to a greater expectation of choice among customers, to which suppliers have had to respond with a greater variety of differentiation, to meet the preferences of progressively more variegated, but smaller groups or segments of customers. Modern technology, in sector after sector, has made it possible to move away from serving a few markets of many customers to serving many markets of few customers.

A glance at the egg counter in a supermarket suggests that some customers want their eggs relatively cheap, others 'free-range' and yet others organic. Moreover for each of these categories there are three sizes, making nine segments in all.

Price as indicator of differentiation

Differentiation clearly affects pricing. Differentiation is the cause, the way it modifies pricing is the effect. That is the general rule. However, there is an interesting exception.

Some offerings are hard to compare with their substitutes. Expert advisers are in that category. Examples are business consultants or people providing a catering service in the client's home, or small service garages. Customers shopping around must either get a personal recommendation from an existing or past client or look for some other indication of quality. Lacking other information, customers often treat the prices charged by various competitors as a proxy for quality. In these special cases, price therefore becomes a means of differentiating, for the simple reason that customers have no other criterion to use. Price becomes part of the cause, as well as part of the effect.

This special case does not invalidate the important principle that a strategy of differentiation has a significant effect on pricing and prices.

Does all this matter?

Some managers have been known to be sceptical about all the points made in this chapter, except that they agree with the need to control costs. They believe that cost control on its own is the key to success, and that nothing else matters.

This is one example of the common tendency to overlook the importance of customers. Effective operating performance is widely taken to be all that matters. Given effective performance, sales and profits must follow automatically. That view has again and again led to disaster. It would be nice to be able to forget customers, because we cannot control them. Yet what might be nice, simply does not work, at least not in the long run. Customers' reactions are never automatic!

Y Limited, a company known to the authors, was in deep trouble. It had ceased to be profitable. It had a fairly narrow range of offerings, all sold to other businesses or public authorities, which included both a 'Rolls Royce' version and a cheap standard version. Neither sold well. Neither was profitable.

A survey was conducted among: (a) all levels of management (b) all customers (c) many potential customers and (d) competitors. The overwhelming view of the internal respondents (a) was that Y Limited's two offerings both competed on price, and the overwhelming view of all three external groups (b)–(d) was that they competed by differentiation, because that was what drove the choices of customers.

Of course, the internal view was not wrong in thinking that cost reduction was desirable, provided it did not reduce the attraction of the offerings in the eyes of customers. However, the managers were seriously wrong if they thought that cost reduction on its own could achieve success, and that no attention needed to be paid to what customers really wanted. This case illustrates why the issue of differentiation matters for real. It is not an airy-fairy theory.

Summary

This chapter has described the nature of a strategy of differentiation and its purpose. Differentiation seeks to attract profitable customers by means of the differences seen by customers between the offering and its nearest substitutes. Its purpose is to make customers choose the offering for its non-price features rather than its price. This gives the company a degree of pricing freedom, some choice between (a) more market share and lower unit margin and (b) more unit margin at less market share and volume.

Differentiation can be in many dimensions and by varying degrees of distance from substitutes. Differentiation matters because it is a prevalent feature of developed markets, and because the preferences of customers are of paramount importance to business success.

The next chapter will draw attention to a very significant and widely neglected dimension of differentiation: the support dimension.

Notes

1. Liu, B. (2004). Krispy Kreme looks to its global roll-out. *Financial Times*, 15 March 2004, p. 15.
2. Penrose, E.T. (1959). *The Theory of the Growth of the Firm*. Oxford: Blackwell, p. 25.
3. Chamberlin describes the nature of pure competition in greater detail. See Chamberlin, E. (1933). *The Theory of Monopolistic Competition*. Cambridge: Harvard University Press, pp. 6–10.
4. Barwise, P. and Meehan, S. (2004). The benefits of getting the basics right. *Financial Times. Mastering Innovation: Part Four*, 8 October 2004, pp. 2–3.
5. Sull, D.N. and Ruelas-Gossi, A. (2004). The art of innovating on a shoestring. *Financial Times. Mastering Innovation: Part Two*, 24 September 2004, pp. 10–11.
6. Vandenbosch, M. and Dawar, N. (2004). Driving value from customer relations. *Financial Times. Mastering Innovation: Part Three*, 1 October 2004, pp. 6–8.
7. Kim, W.C. and Mauborgne, R. (1997). Value innovation: the strategic logic of high growth. *Harvard Business Review*, January–February.
8. Porter, M.E. (1980). *Competitive Strategy*. New York: Free Press.
9. Subject to zero costs of entry, see Baumol, J., Panzar, J.C. and Willig, R.D. (1982). *Contestable Markets and the Theory of Industry Structure*. New York: Harcourt Brace Jovanovich. However, the concept of contestability is valuable even when these costs are not zero.

5

Differentiating in the support and merchandise dimensions

Introduction

This chapter introduces a powerful distinction between merchandise and support as main dimensions in which differentiation can be seen and applied. It also shows how these main dimensions have useful subdimensions. Every specific choice of differentiation represents a different competitive strategy for the new offering.

The chapter then goes on to develop some dynamic applications of these concepts by discussing how differentiation can affect a market area either gently or radically. It can either gently rearrange the area to its advantage or completely transform it, facing customers with an entirely new set of choices.

Another application, the transaction life cycle, illustrates how a market area can oscillate between differentiation and price competition.[1]

The Support/Merchandise Model

We saw in Chapter 4 that there is in principle no limit to the number of dimensions in which an offering can be differentiated. We now, however, come to a distinction between two 'super-dimensions', those of support and merchandise differentiation. That distinction can be a powerful tool.

Those features of an offering which help the customer to choose, obtain and then use the offering, we call support. All other features that customers could see as differentiating the offering, we call merchandise differentiation. The great practical value of these concepts is to counter the widespread tendency to neglect support differentiation. That neglect affects tangible offerings, or 'goods', more than intangible ones, often called 'services'.

Any given model of ink-jet printers, offered for example by Hewlett-Packard under the Officejet name, is clearly a tangible offering. We can treat the quality of its print output, its range of colours, its speed of printing, its interface cable with the PC, the simplicity of its controls as features, which can be differentiated in the merchandise dimension. On the other hand we can treat its instruction book, the availability of technical help with operating problems and the ease with which replacement cartridges are available, as belonging to the support dimension.

However, the idea of support matters equally in intangible offerings. A salon of hair stylists may offer much more than a variety of hair styles to choose from. It may offer more attentive staff, better booking and parking facilities and give advice on the type of hairstyle that would suit customers with a particular physiognomy and instruct them in after-care. Similarly, a clinic offering hernia operations may differentiate itself not in the quality of its treatment – that would be merchandise differentiation – but the fact that it makes access and after-care a more painless experience than its rivals: that is support differentiation, in this case in help with *using* the offering.

The precise borderline between merchandise and support is not always clear-cut, nor is that important. In a restaurant, it does not matter whether explanations of the menu by the staff are treated as merchandise or support. What matters, is the awareness that such explanations can matter to the customer. The support dimension can powerfully affect the reactions of customers. When we design a new offering like a mobile telephone, we should attend to support features and opportunities. At the beginning of the twenty-first century, Nokia's offerings were gaining market share among mobile telephones because they were simpler to use than competing substitutes, but some Nokia customers thought its phones might have been even more successful with better designed instruction books.

Chapter 4 showed that the degree of differentiation of an offering from its substitutes could be measured by its effect on customers' price-sensitivity. A highly differentiated offering will be bought by a comparatively narrow group of customers, who are unlikely to be enticed away from it by a minor difference in price. An offering, on the other hand, which is not greatly differentiated from its substitutes, depends heavily on its price for finding customers.

The Four Main Types of Differentiation

Figure 5.1 shows the four general ways in which an offering can relate to its competing offerings. If customers can see little differentiation in either the support or the merchandise dimension, it is called a commodity-buy; if it is regarded as highly differentiated in both dimensions, then we call it a system-buy. If customers see differentiation as low in merchandise, but high in support, we call it service-buy and in the reverse case a product-buy. The unfamiliar '-buy' part of the labels serves to remind us that all four cases describe how *buying customers* perceive and compare the offering with its substitutes. The labels capture the essential nature of the triangular relationship depicted in Figures 3.1 and 3.2. These are effectively four different types of competitive strategy for a future offering.

These labels also draw attention away from the intrinsic nature of what is sold. Complicated burglar alarm systems could be sold as

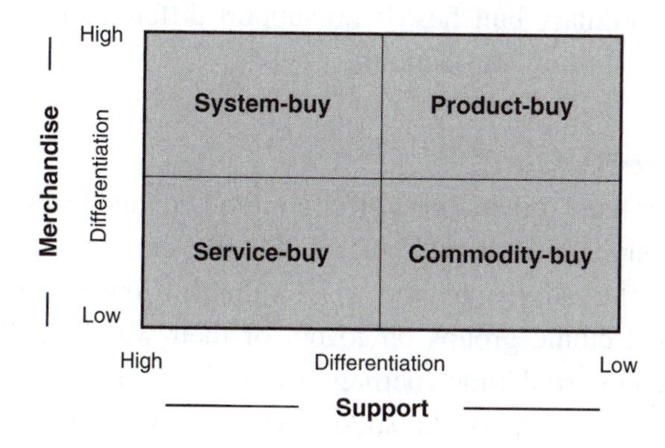

Figure 5.1 Four main types of differentiation

commodity-buys if there was no difference between competing substitutes. On the other hand everyday commodities such as table salt could be sold as system-buys if the salt was perceived as being of exceptional quality and came together with outstanding instructions and advice on its use. Drucker recommended us to see the whole business from the customer's point of view.[2] That aim is greatly assisted by thinking in terms of customer perceptions and using an output-based, rather than input-based vocabulary.

The four cases can apply to any kind of offering, but let us illustrate this again with a tangible offering, because the need for the support–merchandise distinction is less self-evident to many people when it is applied to tangible items or 'goods'.

Flowers: system-buy

Flowers are offered as *system-buy* in shops with prestige names, specializing perhaps in exotic flowers, but also perhaps in a painless ordering procedure and limousine delivery at closely specified times convenient to the recipient. Some shops offer to arrange the flowers on the customer's premises. Differentiation is in both the merchandise and the support dimensions.

Flowers: product-buy

Other shops specialize in exquisite made-up arrangements, which can be placed immediately in a vase as they are, without any work by the recipient. As long as competitors do not match those arrangements, they are clearly differentiated. These arrangements are therefore priced well above ordinary bunches. If no support differentiation is present, this is a *product-buy* transaction.

Flowers: service-buy

On the other hand, other shops offer a more knowledgeable or personalized delivery service to addresses within the local area. For example, they may offer advice on the most suitable flowers for particular religious and ethnic groups or go out of their way to deliver at the customer's preferred time, perhaps even on a Sunday, and to send out a friendly member of the shop's staff. Many shops offer delivery services, but some add these extra courtesies. If the flowers are much like those offered by competitors, this is a *service-buy* transaction differentiated just in the support dimension.

Flowers: commodity-buy

A bunch of cut flowers can in London be bought from numerous shops or street-barrows. A customer wanting to buy a bunch of a certain size can usually choose this or that main colour, or select between various ready made-up arrangements. They are cheapest if flowers in season are chosen. To the extent that all sellers offer these choices and the same support, competition may be mainly on price. That is the *commodity-buy* case. The mere fact of choice does not amount to differentiation, as long as all sellers equally provide it!

Coming Down a Step: Types of Support Differentiation

Figure 5.1 showed the four basic kinds of differentiation. The four cases showed the extent to which the offering is differentiated in either the support or the merchandise dimension. However, these are large categories, and we can refine either of those dimensions by showing two subdimensions in each case.

Figure 5.2 does this for the support dimension. There are two dimensions in which a competitor can differentiate the *support* component of its offering: personalization and expertise.

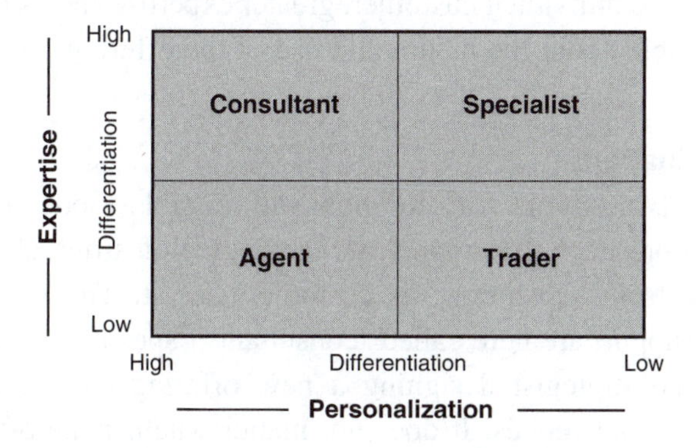

Figure 5.2 Support differentiation – the four modes

Personalization

Personalization is a measure of the pleasing personal attention to each individual customer, perhaps with a special welcoming smile, a cordial handshake, with extra care to ascertain personal circumstances, needs or preferences, or perhaps with the use of the customer's name. Greater personalization does not need to be delivered person to person. More responsive call centres or websites can also achieve it. As always, we measure here the degree to which the attraction of our offering is enhanced by being relatively more personalized than its competing substitutes.

Greater personalization is often a painstaking process. To learn about the individual customer's problems, needs and operating logistics may take rather more effort than a simple questionnaire. That investment may, however, reap rewards that extend far beyond the present offering. The resulting insights can help us to design other successful offerings in the future.

A high degree of personalization can result in considerable customer loyalty. It can also impose switching costs on customers. Both discourage defection to competitors; both make the offering less price-sensitive.

Expertise

The other subdimension of support is expertise. Expertise measures the extent to which customers regard us as proficient in brainpower, talent, skills or experience in specifying, delivering and implementing the offering. Whereas, greater personalization conveys that we know more about the individual customer, greater expertise shows us as more knowledgeable about the nature and use of the offering.

The combinations

Figure 5.2 is a simple way to show the possible modes of support differentiation. Each axis represents the degree of differentiation, that is distance from substitutes, as customers see it. The four possible modes of support are here called 'consultant', 'specialist', 'agent' and 'trader'. The strategist designing a new offering can again choose any of these four modes. It does not matter whether the offering is a Brazilian bond, a bird-bath, a burger or a burglar alarm system.

We illustrate the four modes with Cleanpile and some of its competitors, which make and sell vacuum cleaners and provide support.

Consultant mode

Cleanpile registers all users on a very effective database, so that it can in response to a call greet the user courteously and very quickly identify that user's model and batch numbers and track the service record of that individual cleaner. It can thus instantly diagnose faults reported by users and either advise on how users themselves can remedy them or have its after-sales service team visit with the correct spare parts to fit. From the user's point of view this differentiates Cleanpile's support in both personalization and expertise. It is therefore competing in the consultant mode.

Specialist mode

A competitor, Dirteater, differentiates in expertise, but not personalization. Dirteater users can contact the company with queries, and obtain distinctively expert advice on the best way to tackle different kinds of carpeted areas, as well as on operating problems. Its records of users and their particular needs are no better than those of competitors. Dirteater's support differentiation is in the specialist mode.

Agent mode

Another competitor, Carpfresh, differentiates its personalization, but not its expertise. It keeps particularly efficient records of users and their special requirements and even sends them maintenance tips for their specific models and batches from time to time. However, it refers them to Suctionserve for any servicing or malfunctioning problems. Suctionserve is a vacuum cleaner service company, which services vacuum cleaners made by a number of manufacturers. Carpfresh's support differentiation is in the agent mode.

Trader mode

Finally, our fourth competitor, Flawclear, offers simply the normal level of expertise and personalization in the market. Its support is indistinguishable from that of others. Its lack of support differentiation we call the trader mode.

Vacuum cleaners have served as an illustration, but most offerings can be differentiated – or left undifferentiated – in one of these four support modes.

Types of Merchandise Differentiation

There are also two dimensions in which a business can differentiate the *merchandise* component of its offering by content or by aura.

Content

An offering differentiated by its content would be seen by its customers to have better performance capabilities, or better technical, physical or aesthetic output features than its substitutes. Even the seller's size may add to the attraction of its offerings, if it makes customers feel safer – as in bank deposits – or better able to rely on its reputation, as with Microsoft or Toyota. Content thus distinguishes what the offering will *do* for the customer.

Aura

Aura on the other hand distinguishes what the offering 'says' about the customer, rather than what it will do for him or her. It reassures customers that they have made the right choice of offering, as it will speak well of them, both to themselves and to others. 'It will say the right things about you' is the message conveyed by aura, without specifying any content output features.

Offerings differentiated by aura are often symbols of status and good taste. Apparently there are even literal examples of this. In an article of 12 April 2005, in which there is a reference to 'things that pamper and enhance people's self image' the *Financial Times* reports that in the United States a 7oz tub of Ravida Sicilian sea salt sells for $9, more than 50 times the price of ordinary table salt.[3]

Again, a Patek Philippe Calatrava watch is not bought solely as a means of ascertaining the time. Aura and content may both rely on intrinsic qualities, but they are quite distinct in their function. For example, a Jaeger cashmere pullover may be both more comfortable and more chic than competing ones. Brand names like Prada can convey not just better content, but also better aura.

It does not always take a positive effort by a seller to differentiate by aura. People sometimes prefer a novel offering, as the laptop computer and later the videophone and then the BlackBerry and iPod were at one time, not just for its practical convenience, but in order to impress. Advertising and promotion can of course help to create superior aura, but they have other functions too, such as publicizing better content and support.

Current stress on ethical or socially responsible purchase behaviour can create aura effects. Customers have for this reason turned against the fur trade, against animal experiments in cosmetics and against the offerings of companies believed to have inhumane employment policies in the third world. The damage to such businesses was often due to initiatives from pressure groups. Examples of business responses are as follows:

- Oil companies publicizing their experiments with solar power.
- Body Shop proclaiming that its cosmetics have not been tested on animals.
- Branded training shoes made in the Philippines promoted as made without the use of child labour.

Differentiation of this kind tends to be defensive rather than aggressive. Nevertheless, in some cases it can no doubt serve to win customers, for a while at least, away from unreformed suppliers. In any case, the intended benefit is to the buyer's self-respect. It is a clear case of aura differentiation.

The combinations

Figure 5.3 does for the four combinations of merchandise differentiation what Figure 5.2 did for those of support differentiation. The four modes here are exclusive, augmented, special and standard. In the exclusive case both content and aura are differentiated, in the standard case neither of them is. In the augmented case differentiation is confined to aura, in the special case to content. To illustrate, we again use vacuum cleaners. Interestingly, our four manufacturers have adopted very different stances in the merchandise and support dimensions. It does not in the least follow that Cleanpile, which competes distinctively in both support dimensions, will do the same in merchandise!

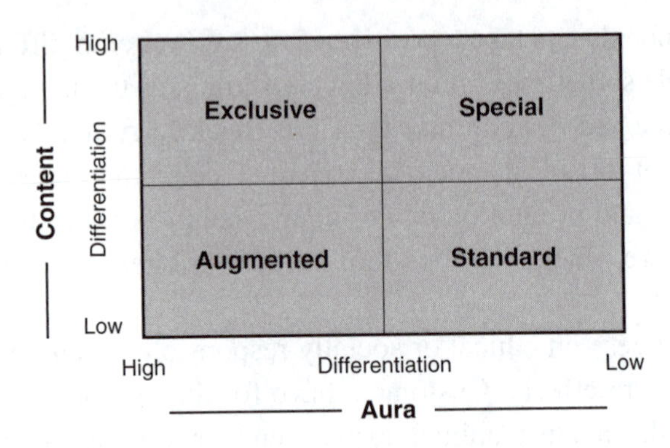

Figure 5.3 Merchandise differentiation – the four modes

It could, but here it does not. Cleanpile is free to adopt any of the possible combinations.

Exclusive mode

Carpfresh differentiates in both merchandise dimensions, content and aura. Customers see it as preeminent in bagless technology with faultless mobility over all surfaces and its brand is well established as the cleaner used by the best people, with special promotions in, say, Harrods a prestigious department store in London. Its mode is the exclusive one.

Special mode

Cleanpile differentiates in content, but not aura. It has fitments specially designed to get into nooks and crannies, and advertises that in some tests by consumer bodies it was found to have the strongest suction and the lowest weight. Its brand name is well respected, but no more than those of its competing brands. That is the special mode.

Augmented mode

Flawclear differentiates in aura, but not content. Its cleaners perform well, but no better than its competitors, but it has established a strong brand with an advertising campaign: *Flawless homes have Flawcleared surfaces*. This resonates with customers and makes them think of themselves as caring homemakers. It thus illustrates the augmented mode.

Standard mode

Dirteater differentiates in neither content nor aura. Its features and its standing are seen to be no worse than those of most of its substitutes, but no better either. In respect of its merchandise dimension it prefers to save cost and to compete on price. This we call the standard mode.

Possible Combinations of Support and Merchandise Differentiation

Of our four vacuum cleaner companies it so happens that none differentiate in all four subdimensions: personalization, expertise, content and aura. As Table 5.1 shows, two of them, Cleanpile and Carpfresh differentiate in three each, the other two in one each.

However, all combinations are possible. When it first hit the market, the Dyson vacuum cleaner alone had the attractive bagless feature (content), it was probably a prestige purchase which impressed others (aura). Dyson had more detailed and better data about the model sold to each user, so as to give each individual the best after-sales service for her particular batch of cleaners (personalization), and it had a distinctively equipped and competent service team (expertise). Dyson thus scored 'yes' in all four columns at that time.

In our scheme, 16 permutations of support and merchandise pairings are possible: any of the four modes of merchandise differentiation can be combined with any of the four modes of support differentiation. These are illustrated in Figure 5.4.[4]

The Dyson bagless cleaner was probably an example of a consultant/exclusive competitor. However, any of these combinations may be successful if skilfully implemented. Some surprising combinations can be very successful: for example, exclusive merchandise with trader or

Table 5.1 Combining modes of differentiation

Name		P	E	C	A
Cleanpile	Consultant/Special	Yes	Yes	Yes	No
Dirteater	Specialist/Standard	No	Yes	No	No
Carpfresh	Agent/Exclusive	Yes	No	Yes	Yes
Flawclear	Trader/Augmented	No	No	No	Yes

Key: P = personalization, E = expertise, C = content, A = aura.

Merchandise \ Support	Consultant	Specialist	Agent	Trader
Exclusive	**System-buy** Consultant/ Exclusive	Specialist/ Exclusive	Agent/ Exclusive	**Product-buy** Trader/ Exclusive
Special	Consultant/ Special	Specialist/ Special	Agent/ Special	Trader/ Special
Augmented	Consultant/ Augmented	Specialist/ Augmented	Agent/ Augmented	Trader/ Augmented
Standard	Consultant/ Standard **Service-buy**	Specialist/ Standard	Agent/ Standard	Trader/ Standard **Commodity-buy**

Figure 5.4 Fuller classification of differentiation

less support. Yet that is what IKEA offers for self-assembly furniture. Buying and transporting purchases home is not a convenient process, and the assembly instructions are not of distinguished quality. In fact what distinguishes them is their capacity for defeating many customers. However, the furniture is chic and stylish at prices attractive to less prosperous, but aspiring customers. IKEA has built much value with it.

These are just two illustrations of the richness of this support/merchandise model.

Applying the Support/ Merchandise Model

The bulk of this chapter has described the support/merchandise model. In this section, we look briefly on how this model can be applied dynamically. We shall here take a bird's eye view of a market area, such as typewriters or vacuum cleaners, so as to see how one novel offering can affect such an area. We shall first contrast radical transformer strategies with less adventurous rearranger ones and then show

how a market area can move from highly differentiated to commodity-buy and back again.

Rearrangers and transformers

Companies designing new offerings can affect the market area of the offering either incrementally or radically. The company which takes the incremental path we call a **rearranger**, the radical company we call a **transformer**.

A rearranger might in the 1970s have introduced golf-ball typewriters, which dispensed with the moving carriage, but it took a transformer to introduce word-processing, which has effectively made typewriters obsolete. The rearranger can make big changes in its market area, but stop short of completely destabilizing it.

The transformer on the other hand destabilizes the market area so violently that the landscape becomes as unrecognizable as after a tsunami: it changes its very definition and composition. Word processing did this for the area previously served by typewriters. So did Japanese motorcycles in the late 1960s. Their cheaper and lighter machines all but displaced the brands which had dominated the market before their entry. Similarly Sellotape ensured that balls of string and a number of other offerings came to something approaching a sticky end.

What distinguishes the transformer from the rearranger is the radical disturbance caused to customer preferences in the surrounding market area. Customers wake up to a transformed landscape. Yesterday there was only one prevailing way to secure a parcel; today the choice is quite different. The transformer often seizes and dominates a virgin market area in which it has no close substitutes.[5]

A market can of course be destabilized by price as well as by differentiation. Japanese motorcycles destabilized markets in the 1960s more by their lower prices than by their differentiated outputs. Heavy discounting in cigarettes forced Philip Morris in 1993 to slash the price of its Marlboro brand so as to regain some lost volume. Wal-Mart destabilized supermarkets by its discounter strategy. At the turn of the century low-cost airlines destabilized the markets of European flag carriers.

A transformer strategy can bring great rewards if the company knows how to catch and keep its competitors off balance. The examples show that this can be achieved not just in leading edge technologies, but also in some apparently much less exciting fields. It can, for example, be applied in adult ice creams, green cosmetics or motor insurance.

The transformer must be able to destabilize as rapidly and as often as is needed. The strategy will be only briefly successful if an original move is easily copied by a rival who enjoys the second mover's advantage: that of learning from the first mover's experience and mistakes. For the right company the transformer strategy can bring rich rewards.

From system-buy to commodity-buy and back again

We now come to the down-and-up-again see-saw pattern illustrated in Figure 5.5 and called the Transaction Life Cycle.

This pattern is common in traditional as well as technically advanced fields. Book retailing in Britain will serve as an illustration. The book trade has seen major change during the twentieth century. Up to and for a few years after World War II books were relatively expensive. Many readers borrowed them from public and private libraries instead of buying them. Fiction has always predominated in this trade. The rise of the paperback greatly cut unit production costs, threatening major change in the structure of wholesale and retail distribution. The trade, however, prevented significant price reductions by persisting with the Net Book Agreement, which outlawed discounting. The NBA did not finally break down until the 1990s. This is the background to our illustration.

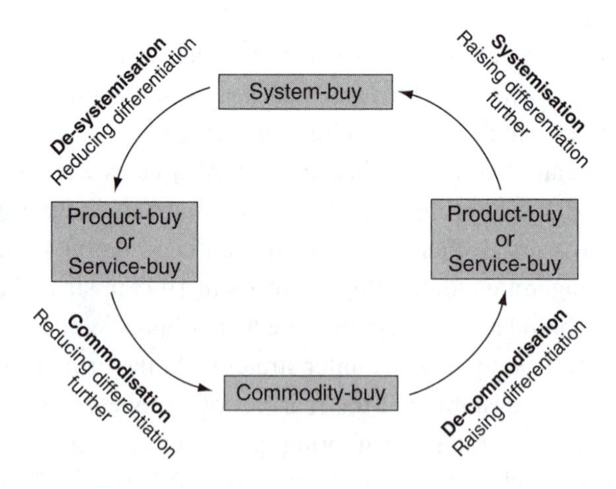

Figure 5.5 The transaction life cycle

Just after World War II there were still relatively few booksellers. A bookseller was often the only one in a locality and faced comparatively little non-local competition. Buyers were the relatively few who loved books and collected them, or wanted to read books not stocked by libraries. Booksellers were often enthusiasts. They offered their customers advice and assistance on the most suitable choice and, if that book was not in stock, procured and delivered it to the customer. Merchandise and support were thus both differentiated: a system-buy transaction.

Had it not been for artificial resistance through the NBA, the rise of paperbacks would have precipitated major change quite early. Buying would have become cheaper compared with borrowing, and the market could have expanded dramatically. In fact paperback editions remained relatively few. Competitive pressures could not, however, be contained completely. The NBA held surprisingly well, but its ultimate weakness was that of King Canute.

An early development was the search for loopholes. Book clubs managed to discount books by requiring a continuing string of purchases with restricted choice for the customer.

As the demand for books grew, so did the competition. Some large sellers opened local branches while others competed by mail order. Local book shops found their near-monopoly progressively declining. This was the de-systemisation phase of book-selling in Figure 5.5. Book clubs competed from a distance. New local bookshops might supply, for example, specialist antique books, yet make little inroads into the business of the existing shop. However, as the number of competitors rose, so did the ways of competing. Some competitors moved closer on the merchandise axis, some on the support, some on both. The degree of differentiation of the pioneer was dramatically reduced. Some outlets provided a larger or more specialized range of books, relying on demand stimulated perhaps by book reviews in journals. Still others offered not different books, but more specialized support aimed at particular groups of customers such as gardeners and schoolchildren. These were the product-buy and service-buy phases of book-selling.

The process of commodisation was thus in place and inevitably ended up by sweeping the NBA away. National chains of book retailers formed, and it was they who openly challenged and ended it. Best-seller novels are now commodity items bought from the Internet or just as easily and cheaply in supermarkets along with cornflakes as well as in bookshops. Competition depends largely on price. All this matured the commodisation process.

However, at almost the same time the Internet brought further ways of differentiating book retailing. Internet sellers give customers more convenient access to their purchases. They provide not only specialized searches, but also more convenient delivery. These are clear examples of differentiated support and of a new process of de-commodisation. Moreover this support is often personalized in that it takes account of a buyer's preferences evidenced by earlier visits to the site. Bookshops, led by some large chains, fought back. They began to lure customers back into the shops by a well-presented and wide selection of books and making the customer's visit a truly pleasurable event. Books can now be bought on premises that resemble libraries and cafés and encourage the customer to browse and sip coffee and consult intelligent terminals and knowledgeable staff. This clearly faces Internet sellers with differentiation which can hardly be matched online. Perhaps it can be described as systemisation and the development of a new type of system-buy. Of course as more and more stores in a particular catchment area adopt this way of competing, they are all doomed to become commodity-buys. That is the nature of active competition.

The lesson from this dynamic process is not the neat symmetry of the sine curve, but the rich variety of possible competitive strategies. Many new offerings begin as system-buys and decline to commodity-buys, but that need not constrain strategists if they can see an advantageous way to reverse the trend at any point. To swim against the tide can be very profitable. Change in markets is governed not by mechanical forces like the 'product life-cycle', but by the initiatives of competitors.[6]

Summary

Chapter 5 has shown that the infinite number of dimensions in which an offering can be differentiated, lends itself to a powerful subdivision into support and merchandise differentiation, with further sub-categories of each of these. The two dynamic patterns of the transformer offering and of the down-and-up-again pattern illustrate how wide the choices are, and how the apparently oddest choice can sometimes be the most successful.

Notes

1. The ideas in this chapter were developed over several years. See Mathur, S.S. (1984). Competitive industrial marketing strategies. *Long Range Planning*, **17**(4), 102–109 and Mathur, S.S. (1988). How firms compete. *Journal of General Management*, **14**(1), 30–57. Also see Mathur, S.S. (1992). Talking straight about competitive strategy. *Journal of Marketing Management*, **8**, 199–217.
2. Drucker, Peter F. (1968). *The Practice of Management*. London: Pan Books.
3. Tomkins, R. (2005). Shop till you stop: the problem of consumer satiety. *Financial Times*, 12 April 2005, p. 13.
4. For a fuller discussion, see Mathur, S.S. and Kenyon, A. (2001). *Creating Value*. Second edition. Oxford: Butterworth Heinemann, p. 100.
5. For more illustrations of such a strategy, see Kim, W.C. and Mauborgne, R. (2004). Blue ocean strategy. *Harvard Business Review*, October, pp. 76–84. Also see Christensen, C.M. (2000). *The Innovator's Dilemma*. New York: Harper Business.
6. For an approach that puts more emphasis on the product life-cycle, see Levitt, T. (1965). Exploit the product life cycle. *Harvard Business Review*, November–December, pp. 81–94.

6

Differentiation creates private markets

This chapter looks more closely at the nature of markets for differentiated offerings. This sheds a useful light on just which competing substitutes compete with an offering.

In What Type of Market Will Our Offering Compete?

For the task of designing new offerings for our company, we need a clear view about the market in which a new offering will compete. That means a clear view about the customers it will target and the competitors it will contest. It helps to think of a market as a communication system in which buyers and sellers can interact and thereby arrive at prices that balance supply and demand.[1]

The simplest kind of market is one in which buyers see competing offerings as completely *undifferentiated*. In such a market, competition is purely a question of price. The competing offerings will settle down at a single price at which the quantities offered by suppliers will be equal to those bought by buyers. That price is called the 'equilibrium' price. It is called that because at that price no party has an incentive to change the quantities it wishes to buy or sell.[2] Examples of such markets are that for spot dollars in London, or the market for Brent crude oil. Let us for now call this a U (for undifferentiated) type market, illustrated in Figure 6.1.

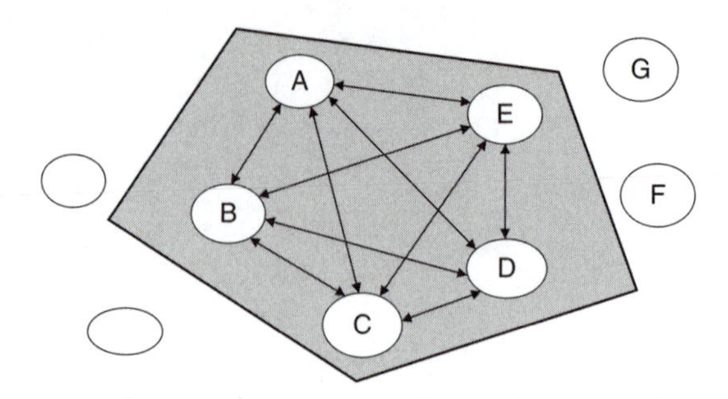

Figure 6.1 Public market of undifferentiated offerings A, B, C, D and E

That simplicity is lost in a D type of market, where offerings are *differentiated* in customers' minds. Differentiation brings two important changes from the U type: (a) in equilibrium there is no single market price and (b) competing substitutes do not have identical sets of customers and competitors: their sets will overlap, but not completely.[3] These important points will now be explained.

First, differentiated competing offerings will not settle down at one single price. In fact each competing offering is likely to have a different equilibrium price. This is because customers will not be willing to pay the same price for all the offerings which they see as substitutes, if at the same time they regard them as differentiated. A typical customer will normally be willing to pay more for substitute x than for substitute y. In their comparison between x and y, they will compare *value for money*. For example, if cup of tea costs 80p, and cup of coffee 75p, they may prefer tea. If the price of a cup of coffee came down to 60p, they might find coffee better value. Perhaps, they would regard them as equal value for money if tea cost 80p and coffee 70p per cup. What matters here is that they are no longer just comparing prices, but value for money. So the differentiated market reaches equilibrium not at a single price, but at a *pattern of prices*.

Secondly, the D type of market is intermeshed with its neighbouring markets. This is in stark contrast to a U type market, which is self-contained. Suppose our offering A has four competing substitutes as in Figure 6.2. That group of five offerings would be A's market, but not B's, C's, D's or E's. None of the other four offerings has *exactly* the same four competitors as A, and no other substitutes. Because they are differentiated, B, C, D and E are each likely to have different

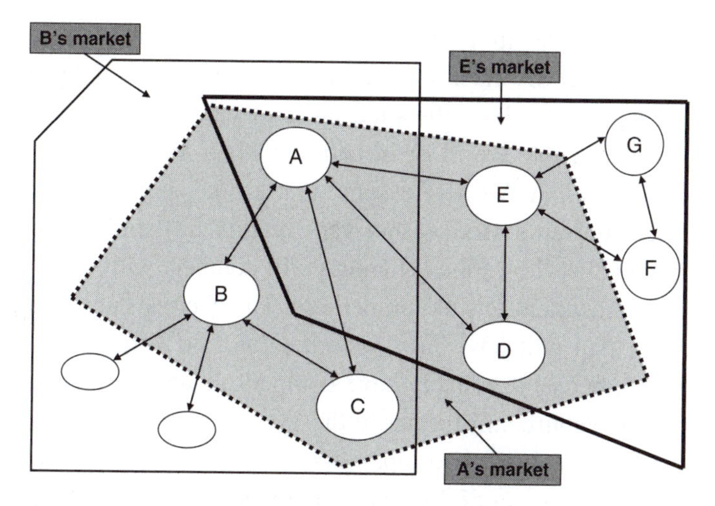

Figure 6.2 Private markets of differentiated offerings A, B and E

competing substitutes outside the A–E group. Figure 6.2 shows this for B and E. By the same token customers do not see B or C as substitutes for D or E. Similarly, E competes with F, but neither A, B, C nor D compete with F. No offering has exactly the same set of substitutes as any other offering from which it is differentiated.

We ought to be a little stricter in our use of words here. When we say that customers do not see C and D as substitutes, we strictly mean that C and D have no *significant* influence on each other's prices. A market is after all a price-determining mechanism. We need that word 'significant', because the question of whether C and D are substitutes or not is in fact a matter of degree, not a simple yes or no question. There may well be some few customers who see them as competing, but not enough to have any practical influence on prices.

Each offering will thus have its own set of substitutes close enough to affect its price. The sets will partially overlap, but none of them will be identical. When an offering has no significant influence on the price of another offering, then those two offerings are not in the same market. If a bottle of vintage champagne does not compete with a bottle of Californian red wine, they are not in the same market. On the other hand if passengers choose between Eurostar trains and airlines on the London to Paris route, then they are in the same market.

This pattern of competition is perhaps easiest to understand where differentiation is mainly one of location. We illustrate this with chemist shops or pharmacies in a typical English suburb. In it chemist shops are dotted all over the map. Some customers will visit them by car, and travel perhaps two miles, others may walk. Chemists are often needed quickly when people are ill or in pain, or when the doctor has given them a prescription. We here assume that all the shops in our suburb offer much the same service, and vary mainly in their location. The effect will be that the various chemists will compete with overlapping, but not with identical sets of competitors. The chemists at the Western end of the map will have few customers and no competitors at the Eastern end, but will probably have competitors and customers in the neighbouring suburb still further to the West of ours. In this way each chemist will have a list of competitors and customers, which to some extent differs from that of the nearest competitor and more from those further away. Figure 6.2 illustrates this.

Location is of course only one of many dimensions in which offerings can be differentiated. The same pattern will apply if the shops differ in other dimensions. For example, local chemists may offer different photography services. One shop may have a film processing service with better colour matches. Another may have the processing equipment on the premises and give a much quicker service. The first differentiates in the merchandise, the second in the support dimension. Each such feature attracts different customers and identifies different rivals. The same pattern applies to cars, holiday tours and virtually all other kind of offerings.

Another obvious example is watches. The watch 'industry' or market is widely defined as including everything: from the Patek Philippe's Sky Moon Tourbillon, which retails for about half a million pounds, to the Rolex Oyster Perpetual Datejust suitable for those whose budget runs to only a few thousands, to the Sekonda Trident available for a few pounds and suitable for those few who still think that the purpose of a watch is restricted to telling accurate time. Yet these watches are not mutual substitutes. Some customers may regard the Omega Seamaster or the Breitling Montbrilliant Chronometer or the Bulgari Classic as a substitute for the Rolex, but not the Sekonda Trident. And of course the Patek Philippe – unlike the Rolex – competes with works of arts and antiques, and the Sekonda with books and cosmetics as a gift fit for young men on the verge of adulthood. Each offering has its own list of substitutes: there is no common list, no group that includes all competitors and excludes all non-competitors.

Public and Private Markets

We can now label the self-contained U type of market in Figure 6.1 a *public* market, and the differentiated D type in Figure 6.2 a *private* market. In the public market competing substitutes are common to all the interested customers, and publicly known. There is a clear dividing line, a discontinuity between offerings that do and do not supply this market. The public market, illustrated in Figure 6.1, is

a. exclusive, because there is no competition across its boundaries;
b. inclusive, because every offering in the market competes with all the others in it and
c. public in the sense of being defined by publicly known boundaries; the list of competing substitutes is widely known.

The D type market, however, has none of these three characteristics. We call it a private market, because each individual offering has a unique set of competitors, even though some of the competitors overlap with those of other offerings in that market, as in Figure 6.2. In that sense the market is private to that specific offering.

When we design a differentiated offering, we should therefore consciously have the pattern of the private market in mind. This is needed to sharpen our awareness of

- the need to identify the customer groups addressed by our proposed offering;
- the need to identify the quite specific substitutes which will to different degrees appeal to those groups;
- the need to use that information to assess the overall effect of these differing counter-attractions on the price we can charge for our own offering in our own private market.

In the modern economy most offerings compete in private, not public markets. When analysts discuss competition as taking place in industries or in sectors or within categories of products or in other groups, it is the model of the public market that they usually have in mind. That model hardly fits the real world of today in which differentiated offerings are increasingly becoming the norm.

Summary

In this chapter we have focused on the markets in which differentiated offerings compete. There are two important differences from those in which undifferentiated offerings compete.

1. The markets establish not an equilibrium price, but an equilibrium system of value for money.
2. The markets are private to each offering, in the sense that each offering has a partially different set of competing substitutes.

The strategist should use these insights to assess just what substitutes a new offering will face, and what degree of latitude there will be for its pricing.

Notes

1. Stigler, G.J. and Sherwin, R.A. (1985). The extent of the market. *Journal of Law & Economics*, **XXVIII**, 555–585. Also see Curran, J.G.M. and Goodfellow, J.H. (1990). Theoretical and practical issues in the determination of market boundaries. *European Journal of Marketing*, **24**(1), 16–28.
2. Lipsey, R.G. and Chrystal, K.A. (1995). *Positive Economics*. Eighth edition. Oxford: Oxford University Press.
3. Chamberlin, E. (1933). *The Theory of Monopolistic Competition*. Cambridge: Harvard University Press, pp. 68–70. Also see Boyer, K.D. (1979). Industry boundaries. In: Calvani, T. and Siegfried, J. (eds) *Economic Analysis and Antitrust Law*. Boston: Little, Brown & Co, pp. 88–106.

7

Markets with dominant players

Introduction

We saw in Chapter 3 that – for its payback period at least – an offering needs to be protected against imitators of its winning position. Otherwise it cannot beat its cost of capital. We mentioned three kinds of protection: differentiation, lower unit costs and market barriers. Protection of the first two kinds mostly comes from winning resources discussed in Part 3 of this book. In this chapter we look at the effects of market barriers. These barriers protect some offerings and threaten others.

Many managers reading the last few chapters may not recognize in them the markets in which their own offerings compete. This may be because so far we have tacitly assumed that our markets are fragmented and open: open in the sense that new entrants can easily come in and compete, and fragmented in the sense that no competitor or group of competitors has a leading or dominant position.

In fact many, perhaps most offerings, compete in markets which are neither open nor fragmented. Managers of such offerings typically watch a mere handful of competitors. They compete in markets dominated either by one player or by a small group of players. The technical economic term for this is 'oligopoly'.[1] Strictly, this pattern applies where there are either

a. few sellers, among which one may or may not be dominant or
b. many sellers, but with a dominant small group, which itself may be dominated by a single leader.

The condition of oligopoly is well described and its changing nature in a world of global competition well explained by Barry Lynn in an article in the *Financial Times* of 14 February 2006.[2] In such a world, consolidation and competition have increased simultaneously. For example, the world's largest traders and retailers have tightened their grip on global marketplaces and used their market power to pit supplier against supplier.

Whenever power is exercised by a group rather than by a single seller, its members are in open or tacit collusion, or at least wary about rocking the boat. Dominance means the power to manipulate prices and impose or maintain entry barriers. Dominance usually brings higher margins. Where the market contains also a number of non-dominant players, the dominant group can largely ignore the minnows.

A defining feature of a dominant group is its interdependence. None of its members, not even the predominant member if there is one, can afford to change its competitive position materially without taking into account possible reactions from the rest of the group. This phenomenon is sometimes called 'circularity',[3] because A needs to watch B and B needs to watch A. Circularity is very common. It applies, for example, to the major supermarket or DIY chains in most countries, to steel manufacturers, to the major oil companies and to the leading international audit firms. It also often applies to local retailers, such as hotels, caterers or greengrocers.

What Causes Dominance by a Small Group?

These conditions result from some barrier that makes entry difficult. Without such a barrier, outsiders could come in and offer better or cheaper substitutes and thus erode the advantage enjoyed by the dominant players.

As an aside, 'entry' is not strictly the best term to use, because that word strictly applies in a public market with homogeneous offerings. When an existing offering is differentiated, the 'entrant' is unlikely to compete in the *whole* of its private market. Hence 'encroachment' would be a better word, but we shall here ignore that technicality.

Barriers have four main sources:

1. regulation by political authorities;
2. selection of suppliers by public authorities;
3. market power exercised by market participants; and
4. 'natural' obstacles to entry.

1. Regulation can, for example, take the form of licensing. In India many activities are still open only to holders of licences from Government. Unless a large number of licences are granted, oligopoly or circularity must result.

2. Public authorities such as central government, local government and state-owned enterprises usually have approved lists of suppliers, often quite short lists.

3. Market participants often obtain dominant positions by controlling key supplies or by acquiring a major market share. Where this power is obtained by a single seller such as Microsoft, it produces domination by a single party. However, in many cases it is acquired by a small dominant group, who are able to keep smaller competitors out as long as none of the group members rock the boat.

4. A 'natural' oligopoly can, for example, arise

a. from economic barriers, such as the need for a large capital investment for entry into airframe manufacture;
b. from geography, for example transport services on a small island; or
c. from the scarcity of some resource, such as sites for large supermarkets in the United Kingdom.

Price Leadership

Where there is a single predominant seller, that seller tends to have price leadership. It has become the price-setter. All the others, inside and outside the dominant group, are to varying degrees price-takers. Price leadership is a most valuable asset. It nearly always ensures superior returns. However, the possible reactions of other members of a dominant group set a limit to the price-setter's freedom to set prices. Minnows on the other hand have little influence.

When Wal-Mart entered the supermarket business as a discounter with a destabilizing variety of goods, far wider than the variety covered by supermarkets at that time, its primary strategic aim was probably market power, to be achieved by price-cutting. Its offering was also differentiated by its much wider variety, especially of non-food items. Nevertheless, its basic strategy was one of price leadership. Wal-Mart was clearly a transformer (Chapter 5) and a price-setter. The circularity of the resulting relationship ensured that Wal-Mart had to stay at some minimum distance below its main rivals' prices, whereas they had to stay within some maximum distance above Wal-Mart's. The dominant group members were interdependent, but Wal-Mart as price-leader had much greater room for manoeuvre than the rest of the dominant group.

Confronting Circularity

Circularity is very common, and arguably the most prevalent environmental feature of competitive strategy, but the rules of the game are psychological rather than economic. Game theory is sometimes used to give it a rational structure, but it may be difficult to find players who behave with the assumed degree of rationality in that environment. It may well be more rewarding to study the psychology of each rival player.

Circularity therefore implies actual or at least potential instability. Unless the barrier is overwhelmingly strong, no player can confidently count on retaining its present margins or market share, even if none of the dominant group upset the apple cart.

Dominant Groups and Differentiation

In Chapters 4–6, we discussed differentiation. In this chapter we are looking at markets with barriers which produce domination and circularity. In fact differentiation and circularity often overlap, as in position X of Table 7.1. Offerings in a restricted market are often differentiated. This makes an appreciable difference. When offerings are undifferentiated as in position W, then the uncertainties of interdependence come in their purest and riskiest form. Leadership can bring high rewards. On the other hand being dominated by others can make our own returns

Table 7.1 Four types of market conditions

	Undifferentiated offerings	Differentiated offerings
Dominant group: circular	W	X
No dominant group: fragmented	Y	Z

very precarious. When our offering is differentiated, it will enjoy at least some protection from the penalties of being dominated. Some customers will prefer our offering, and will thus be less likely to defect to a price-cutting rival.

It is useful to think of markets as being of four kinds, as in Table 7.1.[4]

This chapter describes W and X markets. Previous chapters dealt with Y and Z markets. These four categories help managers to be aware of the four conditions: there either is or is not a dominant group in the market, and in it offerings either are or are not differentiated. In real life the answers are seldom as clear-cut as that, but we still need to reflect on the extent to which there is dominance or differentiation. The answer makes a huge difference to how our new offering needs to be positioned in order to prosper. The British Army has an old maxim: time spent on reconnaissance is never wasted. The strategist needs a similar rule: time spent thinking is never wasted.

Threats Faced by Offerings in a Circular Market

Dominated or circular markets tend to be riskier than other markets, because the stakes are often higher, and because some players have the power to rock the boat. Dominant sellers often earn relatively high returns. Others can enjoy some prosperity, but it is always precarious and at the mercy of other players' decisions.

Circular markets are thus inherently unstable. However, many circular markets retain a particular configuration for long periods, either by coincidence or by cautious inertia. The threats are there, but they do not happen to materialize. These markets are especially treacherous for those who are not aware how precarious that enduring equilibrium actually is. All players in circular markets therefore need to be aware of the threats. These come from breakdowns in the barriers which made the market circular in the first place. For example in the United Kingdom the proposal to allow supermarkets to sell prescription medicines would radically jeopardize the viability of local chemists.

We saw the four main sources of barriers earlier in this chapter. Each of them carries within it threats to the market's stability. Regulatory policy may change, and so may the policies pursued by various sellers.

1. Governments like that of China may come to prefer open competition to regulation. 'Big Bang' did this for the London equity market firms in the 1980s.
2. Public authorities may find it more efficient to open up or change their list of suppliers.
3. A competitor may suddenly decide to rock the boat by starting a price war, as did News International for the London newspapers in 1993.
4. Another competitor may discover a way of entering without heavy investment, or with a new and cheaper material. The local bookseller, travel agent or supermarket may face competition from an online competitor.

It pays to scan the horizon for all these types of threats.

Strategists should be alert to all these different threats, and gather intelligence about possible actions of competitors and authorities. At the same time each barrier or threat has its aggressive flip side: it could be an opportunity for a competitor to upset the apple cart to its own advantage. In other cases an aggressive competitor can manipulate a continuing barrier to its own advantage, for example by finding favour with a regulator or a public purchaser.

Circularity and the Strategist

Success in a circular market depends on whether we have the necessary skills and other assets.

These can include

- scarce decisive factors like prime sites for supermarkets, landing slots for airlines, raw material licences in controlled economies;

- a sustainable technological lead;
- a strong balance sheet, to fund unexpected needs to invest, in response to sudden changes in the market;
- better intelligence about customers and competitors;
- agility in moving to exploit new opportunities or meet new threats; and
- sustainable cost advantages.

Sustainable cost advantages can be absolute, for example a cheaper source of a raw material under our own control, or due to economies of scale and therefore market share. We may be able to create or improve market share by acquiring a competitor, for example, or by aggressive pricing. News International's price war against its rivals in the British national press in 1993 was an example.

Hence, we should consciously adopt one of three approaches when designing a new offering:

1. If we have the necessary advantages, it may pay to actively create or join or remain in circular markets. At best we could aim to become the single dominant player within the dominant group, gaining price leadership.
2. If we lack them, our best approach may be to avoid circular markets.
3. If we have some advantages, but are not quite sure of our superiority, then we should either avoid circular markets or mitigate their effects by differentiation. Any supermarket chain damaged by Wal-Mart's entry could try to escape by targeting a limited, perhaps more affluent set of customers and becoming a profitable niche player. Waitrose is an example in the United Kingdom.

Our conscious choice of one of these approaches may well turn out to be our most important judgement.

Before we adopt a strategy of proactively becoming a dominant player, we should be aware that such a move can bring us into conflict with the public interest. Unlike differentiation, circularity can work against that interest. The risk of running into regulatory obstacles and costs must therefore be heeded. The risk is rather smaller in markets which are not naturally competitive, such as the markets of some utilities. In any case this is a risk to be taken seriously.

As already mentioned, we are sceptical about game theory in this context, because we do not believe that members of dominant groups behave as rationally as game theory assumes. Game theory may lead to valuable theoretical insights, but it is hardly a substitute for the skills, assets and judgements just outlined.

Are Circular Markets Public or Private?

We saw in Chapter 6 that where offerings are differentiated, they each have a private market, with different boundaries from the markets of their competitors, although these markets overlap.

In this chapter we saw that offerings in circular markets can be either differentiated or undifferentiated. If they are undifferentiated, then their markets are of course what we called 'public' ones.

However, what if the offerings are differentiated? Here we get a curious mixture. When a market is characterized by both circularity and differentiation, then

- each offering will still have a private market with a different (though partially overlapping) list of substitutes from its neighbours. That is the consequence of differentiation;
- the group which is protected by entry barriers is public in the sense that its members are known, and circularity applies between all of them, and not to any offerings outside it. A move by any member of the group may affect all the others. That is the consequence of circularity.

Managers need not pay too much attention to this complex technical point, but should be aware that private markets can in this type of case look like public ones!

Summary

Markets with a dominant group, with or without a single predominant party within that group, are very common. The cause is the existence of some barriers limiting entry by competitors. In such a market none of the members of the group can change their competitive positions without heeding possible reactions by the others. This feature has been called circularity. It induces an element of potential or actual instability.

Strategists should

- be aware of the various types of barriers and what might create or remove them;
- study the conduct, capabilities and psychologies of the other members of their present and future group; and
- carefully assess their own company's assets and skills in exploiting or managing the higher risks of such markets, and judge whether they wish to enter or remain in markets where the stakes are so high; success can yield high returns, failure can bring steep penalties.

Differentiation is commonly found in circular markets. It tends to mitigate the effects of circularity by providing a measure of insulation. With a differentiated offering the decision to enter or remain in such a market becomes somewhat less aggressive.

Circularity is one of the critical issues of competitive positioning. It characterizes many, perhaps, most customer markets. A manager needs to understand it in order to assess the opportunities and threats facing the competitive position of any proposed new offering in such markets.

This concludes Part 2 with its review of winning competitive positions. Part 3 will deal with companies' winning resources.

Notes

1. Lipsey, R.G. and Chrystal, K.A. (1995). *Positive Economics*. Eighth edition. Oxford: Oxford University Press.
2. Lynn, B. (2006). Wake up to the old-fashioned power of the oligopolies. *Financial Times*, 14 February 2006, p. 17.
3. Triffin, R. (1940). *Monopolistic Competition and General Equilibrium Theory*. Cambridge: Harvard University Press.
4. Based on Ibid.

PART 3

No Success Without Winning Resources

An offering cannot be expected to generate value unless it exploits both

a. a favourable competitive position vis-à-vis customers and competing substitutes and
b. the seller's very own winning resources.

Part 2 discussed how we could find a winning competitive position. Part 3 addresses the issues of winning resources. Chapter 8 describes the four cornerstones which are needed to make a resource a winning one, Chapter 9 discusses the pitfalls that have misled managers in this connection, and Chapter 10 sums up how winning competitive positions and winning resources are in practice combined to design a value-creating offering.

8

A winning offering needs to exploit winning resources with the four cornerstones

Introduction: Winning Resources Are Needed for Sustained Value Building

We begin by recapitulating the financial requirements of success set out in Part 1. For a new offering to create value, its expected cash flows, discounted at its own risk-adjusted rate of return, must have a positive NPV. This we saw in Chapter 2.

The new offering must therefore do a lot better than break even, and it must do that in cash, not in accounting terms. It must earn a cash surplus appreciably *better* than the return expected by the financial markets. That rate of return is also called its cost of capital. Moreover, those returns must be robust and sustained enough to achieve a positive NPV.

The cash history of the offering begins with the investment in it. That represents cash *outflows* carrying little or no discount, because they occur early. These cash outflows must be made good by subsequent more heavily discounted and therefore larger net inflows. They need to be *sustainable* at least until the cumulative value built by the offering turns positive. That 'payback' period varies with the logistics of each offering. We illustrated this in Figure 2.1 in Chapter 2.

All this is quite a challenge, and companies often come to grief because their offerings fail to stay the course. There are many reasons for this. Glitches occur on the operating side when costs are not well controlled, or when distribution or sales management falls short of best practice. They also, however, occur in operationally efficient companies for two reasons. First, offerings may have been designed merely to do no better than break even in accounting terms, rather than to beat their cost of capital. Secondly, they may have been badly chosen or designed. Failures often come from predictable moves by competitors or from predictable reactions of customers, or even from shifts in customer preferences which occur irrespective of what is on offer from competing sellers.

When we design a new offering, we need to take account of the natural responses to its launch by old and new competitors. Some offerings fail because competitors have simultaneously planned similar or better substitutes. However, suppose our new offering is immediately successful and is seen to generate value. In that case our offering becomes a magnet to emulators. Others are sure to seek similar lush returns by imitating our offering and competing with it. Examples are legion. The success of Body Shop encouraged retailers like Boots in the United Kingdom and Bath & Body Works in the United States to offer their own lines of green cosmetics. In the United Kingdom, Direct Line was followed by other direct sellers of motor insurance. Dyson's bagless technology for vacuum cleaners attracted competitors such as Hoover. Häagen Dazs led Ben and Jerry and others and also supermarkets to offer luxury ice creams. The success of Viagra begot competitors such as Levitra. Just as nature abhors a vacuum, so our lush returns act as a powerful magnet to old and new competitors. If they successfully ape our offering, its sales or its price or both of them will decline and so will our returns, quite possibly before it has beaten its cost of capital. This inevitable market tendency we need to forestall. Either we need a faster payback or we have to make the new offering imitation-proof for long enough. That is one of the reasons why we need *winning resources*: resources which are peculiar to our company, hence not available to others, and which

a. generate the required positive cash flows; and
b. sustain that value generation long enough to recover the cost of capital.

Of course, any resource is an asset like any other. The opportunity cost principle therefore applies to it. If any positive value, which it can build for our company in new offerings, is less than the cash for which we can sell it, then we must sell it.

This chapter describes the four characteristics, called cornerstones, which are needed for a winning resource. However, first let us recapitulate the main points just made.

- Winning offerings are rare, because they need to do better than the financial markets require.
- To do that, they must employ winning resources.
- Winning resources are rare, and specific to the company that owns them. The specification of a winning resource needs to be a tough one.
- The toughest requirement is that their winning characteristics must be sustainable against inevitable attack for the entire payback period, which can be a considerable number of years.
- Even a winning resource must be sold if the proceeds are greater than its internal value to the company in producing one or more offerings.

The Basic Case for Winning Resources Is Quite Simple

In Chapter 1, we used the illustration of Phoebe, a redundant financial manager. She decided to set up as a consultant, and commonsense prompted her to look for both a potentially winning position and her own winning resources for the purpose of choosing a specific field in which to set up as a consultant.

That example was of course far too simple. The mere fact that Phoebe has experience of social responsibility issues was not enough to constitute a winning resource. The example merely served to show that the twin requirements of a winning market position and a winning resource are no more than commonsense, not a far-fetched counsel of perfection.

Resources, Capabilities and Competences

For a resource to be a winning one, it needs to give a competitive edge to one or more *individual offerings.* A software system which enables a company to calculate, agree and pay its tax at much lower administrative cost is a *valuable* resource, but not a winning one.

In order to give that competitive edge to individual offerings, a winning resource needs to meet four conditions or 'cornerstones'. These cornerstones are set out in the next section.

Resources are of many kinds, and benefit a company at many levels. A 'resource', after all, represents any accumulated stock of unexhausted and continuing value. A high-level resource might be a flair for organizing a large and complex company. Its competitive benefit to any one offering might be relatively slight. It is not likely to be a winning resource. Another high-level resource might be Pfizer's research capability for designing successful new drugs. This capability might well characterize the entire company. It might be called Pfizer's core competence, because it is central to all its main offerings. It is also essential to each drug, and therefore potentially a winning resource. There are also lower-level resources, which benefit only one or a few offerings, such as the reputation for high quality of ICI's Dulux brand of paints. This last is of course a mainstream candidate for being a winning resource.

The stress, however, is here on the fact that *any* resource may turn out to be a winning resource if it meets all four requirements in benefiting individual offerings. It does not matter what level resource it is, or whether it qualifies for all-embracing labels like capability or competence or core competence or even more specific ones such as patents, intellectual property or supply chain management skills. We later see that certain categories of resources, such as collective skills and experience, are more likely to be winning ones than others, but in principle any resource could be a winning one.

The benefit of a winning resource can operate at any point of an offering's value chain. The value chain covers all processes in the generation of an offering, from purchasing materials or components to selling and delivering to customers and after-sales service.

When Is a Resource 'ours'?

Throughout our discussion of winning or other resources we briefly refer to 'the company's' resources, and sometimes we speak of such resources as 'owned' by the company.

In fact it does not matter so much whether a company legally owns a resource. For example, most resources that concern us here are the knowledge, skills and even routines of its employees, and a company does not own its employees except where slavery is legal and practised. What really matters is whether a company has some degree of *control* over a resource. The extent to which that is the case is not necessarily linked to ownership. However, it is convenient shorthand to use the language of ownership: otherwise we could not speak of 'the company's' resources. However, the acid test is control, not formal title.

The issues and degrees of control are not a simple matter. A valuable and unique site may well be both owned and controlled. The skills of a single individual may be neither owned nor controlled by the company, except to the extent that the individual has an incentive to remain with the company and resist poachers. On the other hand, knowledge, skills and routines embedded in a team of people may be quite difficult to entice away from a company, and may in that case be considered to be within the company's control to a substantial extent. We shall from time to time come across these complexities.

The Four Cornerstones of a Winning Resource

A number of business gurus have developed the 'resource-based view' which put forward the message we describe in this chapter.[1] One of these writers, Margaret Peteraf, has formally set out the four **cornerstones** or conditions which are needed for a resource to be a winning one.[2] The cornerstones can overlap in their scope: they are not mutually exclusive.

We now adapt and describe those cornerstones using less formal names than those used by Peteraf.

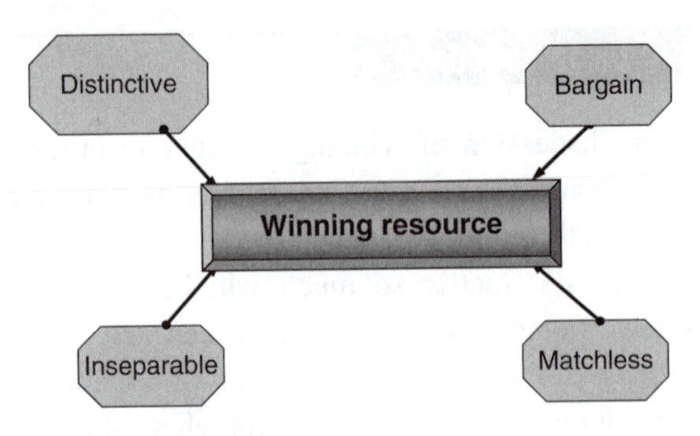

Figure 8.1 The cornerstones that characterize winning resources

As illustrated in Figure 8.1, to be a winning resource the resource needs to be

1. *Distinctive*: It must not be a resource equally available to others. It must be unique to our company, it must be scarce and enable us to market one or more future offerings as either cheaper or more attractive, and thus to earn better than normal returns.
2. A *bargain*: We must not acquire the resource at a cost which equals or exceeds its entire value to the company – in the offering under review and other offerings. Hence we must not pay out the whole of that value to a seller of the resource or in the process of creating it internally. We must, for example, seek to avoid an auction for it. It follows that the market in which it is to be acquired needs to be less than fully competitive. This condition is most easily met where the company already owns the resource.
3. *Matchless*: It must not be capable of being imitated, replicated or replaced by equivalent resources before it has earned the required value in the proposed new offering. It must be imitation-proof and bypass-proof during its entire payback period, that is until the offering is expected to attain a positive NPV.
4. *Inseparable*: It must not during that payback period be vulnerable to poaching, nor must its *value* be capable of being appropriated by powerful employees, suppliers, distributors or other insiders closely connected with the resource.

These four cornerstones will now be described in detail.

Why These Four Cornerstones?

The key cornerstone is *distinctive*. Possession of the resource must distinguish us from our competitors and give us an edge over them. The other three cornerstones serve either to enable the offering to build value or to ensure that we keep our distinctive edge long enough to recover our cost of capital. All four require a degree of imperfection in the market for the resource. Others must not be able to acquire the resource itself or an identical or equivalent resource at an equally advantageous cost.

Distinctive

This is, as just noted, the fundamental cornerstone. The resource-based view came about because analysts wanted to explain how and why some apparently similar companies performed better than others. The answer was that companies were endowed with different scarce resources, and that some of these resources evidently could not be replicated or purchased by others in the market.[3] However, the critical point was that the resources had to be superior in earning power and unique to the company.

Distinctive resources must therefore have three qualities:

a. They must produce offerings which are either (i) extraordinarily attractive to customers, or (ii) deliverable at extraordinarily low unit costs.
b. They must be scarce, that is have few, if any, substitutes that might produce offerings regarded by customers as competing.
c. They must be unique to the company.

Those latter two qualities are of course closely linked with the matchless and inseparable cornerstones, but the fundamental insight is that companies have different resource endowments. That is, what makes them different. Pharmaceutical giant A may excel at research and development, its rival B may excel at marketing and at winning acceptance for a new drug. However, let us look more closely just at R&D. A may be best at fundamental research. C may excel at concentrating research effort on what the market will be eager to buy. Finally, D may be no better than the others at specifying new drugs, but it has an R&D team with a superior collective skill for telescoping the time taken to bring a new drug from first design to regulatory approval to market launch. Each of the four companies has a unique company-specific resource. All these are potential winning resources.

The need to see the resource in terms of how customers see its fruits cannot be overstressed. Suppose we have a unique site for a multimedia shop in central Birmingham, then competitors cannot hope to compete with us for those customers who might be potential customers there. Not, that is, unless that site has now become hard to visit through parking restrictions and other traffic developments, or if a competitor has found a way to reach that customer group rather better via a website. The resource has to be scarce in terms of its *customer pulling power*, not in terms of its physical nature!

A resource can of course be anything, like a company's reputation. However, in order to be winning ones, distinctive resources are usually human skills, and especially collective or team skills. Rouse and Daellenbach have recorded a very useful example of a winning resource.[4] A company was about to outsource its deliveries, when its consultant by sheer chance discovered that the in-house team of delivery drivers were the winning resource of an important offering. The drivers had bonded with customers to the point where this bonding forged customer loyalty. The usefulness of this example will become clearer as we review the other cornerstones. The importance of such collective or team skills is so great that we shall have to return to that theme a number of times.

However, winning resources are not invariably human. They can very occasionally also be inanimate. An example might be a precious site in Rome's Via Veneto or London's Bond Street, which can be owned only by one retailer. However, few inanimate physical assets are sufficiently scarce and superior: that is why most winning resources are human skills or experience. Moreover, human skills are more likely to constitute winning resources if they are *collective*, which means embedded in teams rather than individuals.

Bargain

The value of the resource to the company must not be swallowed up by the cost of acquiring it. Hence the resource must either be in the company's control at the outset, or be obtainable for less than its value to the company. When a get-up-and-go manager gets the message that success cannot be achieved without winning resources, her first reaction might well be to say, 'Right! Let's go and buy some winning resources!' This bargain cornerstone unfortunately puts a firm stop to that keen but over-simple response. It is not as easy as that. Suppose we are a supermarket company, and we decide to go for a unique site for sale in the main street of a Cincinnati suburb. A bank has just taken over a mutual and no longer needs two places of business in that main street, and puts one on the market. This is a unique window of opportunity. However, our supermarket company is likely to find that several competitors and a couple of other banks would also like that site, and an auction develops. Suppose we win the auction and acquire the site. We are only too likely to find that the $7 million price we paid is no less than the site's NPV to us of $7 million. The whole of the value of the resource has been paid to the seller, and none of it stays with us. Neither is it uncommon for auctions to be won by those who overestimate the value of the asset and thus overbid, hence the term 'winner's curse'.[5] The practical message of the bargain cornerstone is that there must not be an auction for the resource.

A second example might be managers of major European soccer clubs. There is in the early twenty-first century a persistent shortage of top-class managers and keen competition for them. The top managers are in strong demand and fairly mobile. The fortunes of any top club or would-be top club may well depend on who selects, trains and manages the teams. On the face of it, an auction is very much on the cards, especially for the top few names in the management world. So should an aspiring club avoid going for a top name? The answer is not simple. On the one hand, payback periods can be fairly short if a new manager is really successful. On the other, managers cannot be tied to a club and can be poached by rivals. Yet pay is not their sole criterion. They too have preferences for specific clubs or even locations. So there are limits to how competitive the market is. Again, no top manager is an exact replica of any other and the chemistry between team and manager varies with each manager. It is very important to obtain one of the handful of top managers, but manager A may be in greater demand than manager B. The risk of an auction may be greater in A's case. So the bargain issue is important in this example, but far from simple.

In both these examples the resources (the site and the managers) are well known. However, many cases are different. Our third example belongs to the category of complex collective skills and routines. We have already referred to the case above, documented by Rouse and Daellenbach, of the company that came close to outsourcing its deliveries to customers, until it was almost accidentally discovered that its team of delivery drivers was the secret of its success.

What distinguishes the delivery team from the site and the football managers is that the resource

- was already within the company's control;
- consisted of the *collective* skills and routines of a team, and was therefore (a) much harder to poach and (b) much less visible, even to its own management!

This team resource may also thrive differently in different companies and their cultures. Even if the whole team were poached, its value may not survive the transplant. If not, it would be a bargain for the company, but not for the poacher.

The delivery drivers are already with the company, but even if they were not, it is unlikely that an auction could develop in this kind of resource, because it is a team. There could hardly be a perfect or near-perfect market in such a team. The imperfection of the market that bargain requires is important in the other cornerstones too. However, when we come to look at the inseparable cornerstone, we shall note that the value of such a team may still be vulnerable to pay demands from the team members themselves.

Bargain asks how we come to *acquire* a resource. The biggest question is whether we already own and control the resource when we design a new offering, or whether we must still obtain it. If we already control it and can prevent others from obtaining it, then the bargain requirement is met. The question then is whether the resource fails other cornerstones.

The main practical effect of bargain is that we must seek to avoid an auction, and even any resource vulnerable to an auction. The outcome of an auction is not foreseeable. What we should in practice shy away from is any resource which gives rise to competition mainly in terms of price. The more the mobility of the resource depends on the price offered to lure it away, the smaller is the chance of avoiding an auction.

We have seen what factors determine this issue of price-sensitivity. They include the value and scarcity of the resource, its visibility, its mobility between companies, its closeness to substitutes and its complexity. If the resource is human, then its mobility is affected by whether it subsists in just one person or a team. The market in a less mobile resource is less likely to produce an auction.

We have noted that if the resource is already owned and controlled, then the bargain cornerstone is met. It is controlled if the company has the power to withhold it from other parties. That prevents an auction for it. In that case it does not matter at what past cost we originally acquired it, only what value it can build in the future. We own and control it by *luck*, because we obtained it without knowing what value it might generate for us in the proposed new offering.[6] Of course, if the resource, which we already own would create *even more* value for us if we sold it, then we should sell it. In that case the value it can build in an offering is less than its opportunity cost. This point was made at the beginning of this chapter.

On the other hand, if we do not already own and control the resource, then we must still acquire it as part of the project to invest in a new offering. We can pay more than others and still meet the bargain condition only through *superior foresight*, that is

1. *either* we have correctly assessed that the resource has in fact a greater NPV to us than to any other business
2. *or* we *and we alone* have correctly assessed the full value of the resource.

Superior foresight works extremely rarely, because it can only operate if all the following three conditions are met:

1. the resource must be available to be acquired, perhaps by purchase or investment or by takeover of the business now owning it;
2. we must *either* be cleverer at spotting its value than others *or* have a uniquely more valuable use for it, unknown to the seller and other interested parties; and
3. the resource must not lose its value to us by virtue of its acquisition, as might happen if the expert team that we are after will defect after our takeover.

If any of them were not met, neither is this cornerstone.

Hence in an overwhelming majority of cases we cannot *set out* to acquire a winning resource. We must already own it. Unfortunately, it is not at all easy to spot our existing winning resources. More of that in Chapter 10.

Matchless

Of all the cornerstones, matchless is perhaps the easiest to understand, though not necessarily the easiest to comply with. The resource must not only help in attracting customers but also be matchless, so that competitors cannot either replicate it, or bypass it with a substitute which will do its job just as effectively.

If our new offering is evidently a winner, it is certain that others will try to follow us down that road, and to market a very similar offering, eroding our prices and margins in the process. If any such attempts were to succeed, our value-generating returns may not persist long enough to achieve the positive NPV we need. The purpose of matchlessness is to make the success of our offering *sustainable*. It aims to make the resource on which the offering depends both (a) imitation-proof and (b) bypass-proof.

Imitation here refers to the imitation of the resource itself; say the site in Central Birmingham that we looked at earlier, by finding another equally effective site. Bypassing refers to achieving the same attraction to customers by another resource, as the Internet website in that example. It is worth contrasting the two processes, as long as we remember that we are really concerned to prevent a single thing: the achievement of the same attraction to customers, whether by the same kind of resource or by any other kind of resource. The scarcity of the site is not enough. It and whatever makes the resource possible to bypass must both be scarce.

A resource cannot be imitation-proof if there is a free market in it. Let us look at some types of obstacles to such free markets. Perhaps the most effective obstacle is sheer *obscurity*. If competitors cannot identify the resource, they also cannot copy it. In the case of the delivery drivers who bonded with customers, the company itself, let alone its competitors, failed to recognize the key role played by this bonding. Even if competitors knew about the extra customer loyalty achieved by the company, they still could not discover its cause. The bad news is of course that many of the most successful resources are so unobtrusive that the company itself has difficulty pinpointing them.

Some obstacles are 'natural', that is external to the company. Others are internal to the company. Internal ones are clearly resources of the company. External ones are not normally what we call resources, but in circular markets (Chapter 7) they can sometimes act much like resources. We return to these in Chapter 10.

All these obstacles we called 'protective armour' in Chapter 3. Obscurity is an example of such armour.

The second example of protective armour is a resource which is *embedded in a team*, like the delivery drivers mentioned earlier, especially if the skill is complex. Complex *collective* skills and routines are, as we have seen, harder to copy than simple ones or those of an individual. Incidentally, the teamwork element also makes the resource much harder to poach. That kills one of the two threats counteracted by our last cornerstone, inseparability.

Another example is the *time* factor. It takes time to acquire the collective skills and routines just discussed.[7] Crash programmes may successfully teach us how to sell apples from a market stall, but cannot train a surgical team to work together in a coordinated and skilful way. A long lead-time too is a form of protective armour.

A fourth example can result from *complementarity* of skills. A physiotherapist in private practice can gain local market share by combining superior diagnostic skills with unusually good contacts in hospitals which introduce new clients. If this combination is not readily imitable by other local physiotherapists, then it can be an armour constituting the matchless cornerstone.

Now for examples of sellers with a capacity for marketing substitutes which bypass the resources of their competitors – we call this the bypass case. The bypass case yet again reminds us that it is what resources do for customers that matters, not their intrinsic nature. IBM may have regarded its golf ball technique for typewriters as unique and scarce, but in fact IBM of all companies needed to think of computers with word-processing software as substitutes.

It is not enough for resource A to be unique and scarce, if a competitor, using other resources, such as B or C produces an equally attractive substitute offering that meets the same customer preference. In our example, the golf ball technique and process may be unique to one supplier, but if there are equally attractive word-processing offerings, the golf ball capability does not meet the matchless requirement.

Again, one of Waterstone's responses to the success of Internet booksellers has been its large bookstore in Piccadilly, London W1, which carries a very large and wide-ranging stock of books at low prices in a store with coffee shops, restaurants and armchairs in which customers can read books to their hearts' content. It has substituted the attractive and convenient physical environment for the ease and convenience of Internet purchasing without leaving one's home. Its prices are competitive with the low prices on the Internet. Waterstone's have successfully found a substitute for the Internet.

The need for matchless varies with the payback period. A very short payback period would greatly reduce the need for it. In Britain over the turn of the millennium automatic car washes were progressively replaced by hand car washes. Suppose Autoclean opened one of these hand car washes with minimal investment, and a resource of dedicated and hard-working family staff. That move might well beat the cost of capital very rapidly, and before others came in to compete with it. In that case matchless was a minor requirement and easily met. The resources were evidently not matchless to any great extent, for in Britain this market became quite competitive within a few years, with aggressive pricing. The lesson here is that the length of the payback period is the key to matchless. Autoclean's success was due more to its short payback period than to the extra quality of its labour resource.

Inseparable

Whereas matchless stops others copying or bypassing our resources, the inseparable cornerstone stops them poaching the resource itself or appropriating its value.

Suppose the company with the attentive delivery drivers had been so small that it needed only one delivery driver who had an exceptional technique for creating customer loyalty. Then a competitor who happened to spot this resource might attempt to poach this driver with an offer to double his or her pay. That is the poaching case.

Poachers are by no means always competitors. The team of delivery drivers might be just as much coveted by a company in a very different business, but with a similar delivery task and a similar need for customer loyalty. An unusually skilled IT expert at a bank may be poached by Oxford University and a reputable chef at a London restaurant by a foreign embassy. Resources can be objects of rivalry in their own right.

Protection against poaching is, as we have seen, a question of the degree of the company's control over the resource. For example, resources which reside in the collective brains of a team are better controlled than those which reside in individuals.

Poaching is one threat counteracted by this cornerstone. The other is appropriation of value. This second threat is not external, but from the inner team of our own employees and others, such as closely related customers or suppliers. It might occur if it dawned on a company's *single* delivery driver that their attitude was the reason why the company was exceptionally successful in retaining customers. In that case they could threaten to defect to a competitor unless their pay was doubled. By means of that threat they might 'appropriate' for themselves their entire value to the company. The company would lose the entire value of the resource to them.

It is not easy to find armour to make the resource appropriation-proof: non-competition clauses in contracts of employment are notoriously hard to enforce by legal action. Of course if the driver were the owner's sister, she might be unpoachable. Such a personal bond might be a powerful illustration of inseparability. This whole illustration also shows why winning resources are much more likely to be found in *collective* or *team* skills and routines than in single individuals. A team is harder to poach or to organize for hard bargaining.

The risk of appropriation, it is worth noting, is an important threat to many resources that pass the *bargain* test. The skills and routines that typically meet the bargain cornerstone may subsist in people who become conscious of their importance to an offering, and exploit it to press for improved rewards.

Another example of such a threat from employees is a private hospital specializing in brain surgery, which may be heavily dependent on the skills of its specialized surgeons or its intensive care nurses. Either of these groups may have the power to appropriate the value of the offering. However, the threats are not in fact just from employees. They may come from any insider, for example from customers, suppliers or subcontractors. A large retailer who is the sole customer of a manufacturer of ladies' hosiery may be able to appropriate the value of any efficiency gains resulting from a revolutionary manufacturing process.

Inseparable, like matchless, serves as armour to maintain the value-building capacity of the resource during the offering's payback period. The threats against which it protects the resource are less of a risk to an offering with a very short payback period.

Summary: The Four Cornerstones

A resource, like any other asset, must be sold if the proceeds of sale would exceed its NPV to the company, in all the offerings likely to benefit from it.

A resource is a winning one only if it has all four cornerstones. The central one is the need for the resource to be *distinctive*, something unique to the company. It also needs to be a *bargain*, which means that we must not pay to the party that sells it to us the whole of its value to us. The other two serve the purpose of making the value of the resource durable for the payback period of the offering concerned. Hence in the rare case where an offering has a very short payback period, these two cornerstones are less important. However, if the resource is not *matchless* or not *inseparable* – in both senses of that latter word – for the duration of the payback period, then it is too vulnerable to be a winning resource.

The combination of these four conditions is not easily met. The next chapter will review some practical problems.

Notes

1. See for example, Barney, J.B. (1991). Firm resources and sustained competitive advantage. *Journal of Management*, **17**(1), 99–120. Also Grant, R.M. (1991). The resource-based theory of competitive advantage. Implications for strategy formulation. *California Management Review*, Spring, 114–135.
2. Peteraf, M.A. (1993). The cornerstones of competitive advantage: a resource-based view. *Strategic Management Journal*, **14**, 179–191. Also see Peteraf, M.A. and Bergen, M.E. (2003). Scanning dynamic competitive landscapes: A market-based and resource-based framework. *Strategic Management Journal*, **24**, 1027–1041.

3. Rumelt, R.P., Schendel, D. and Teece, D.J. (1991). Strategic management and economics. *Strategic Management Journal*, **12**, special issue, Winter, 5–29.
4. Rouse, M.J. and Daellenbach, U.S. (1999). Rethinking research methods for the resource-based perspective: isolating sources of sustainable competitive advantage. *Strategic Management Journal*, **20**, 487–494.
5. John Kay states this occurred in the auction of offshore oil blocks by the US government. See, Why the winner's curse could hit complex finance. *Financial Times*, 23 January 2007, p. 15.

   Kay makes a useful distinction between common value auctions and private value auctions which has a bearing on the nature of foresight discussed later in this section. He writes, 'In a private value auction, as at Sotheby's or Christie's, different bids are the result of different personal preferences for a painting or piece of furniture of agreed specification. In a common value auction, different bids are the result of uncertainty about the real nature of the object and if everyone had the same information all bids would be the same.'
6. Barney, J.B. (1986). Strategic factor markets: expectations, luck, and business strategy. *Management Science*, **32**(10), 1231–1241.
7. Dierickx, I. and Cool, K. (1989). Asset stock accumulation and sustainability of competitive advantage. *Management Science*, **35**(12), 1504–1511.

9

Winning resources: Pitfalls

Introduction: Temptations to Oversimplify

Chapter 8 described the four cornerstones, all of which are needed to make a resource a winning one. In this chapter we look at some practical implications.

Good managers develop a talent for approaching any task by reducing it to its simplest terms. Simplicity makes for clarity and for good communications. Unfortunately, successful competitive strategy cannot be made as simple as most of us would like. Managers can therefore be tempted to cut corners: to oversimplify and to overlook or downplay some awkward, but unavoidable difficulties. This may be one explanation why so many strategies fail to create value.

This natural desire to cut corners results in some pitfalls. In our present context of winning resources they include the following:

1. Going for *any* resources, instead of focusing on winning ones with all four cornerstones.
2. Ignoring the least glamorous of the cornerstones: bargain.
3. Forgetting the most basic cornerstone: distinctive.
4. Underestimating the significance of inevitable efforts of determined encroachers to muscle in on successful offerings, and thus the need for matchless and inseparable.
5. Taking a cavalier approach to matchless and inseparable or to the payback period for which these need to be effective.

6. Underestimating the difficulty of identifying one's own company's winning resources.
7. Ignoring the opportunity cost principle.

We shall now look at each of these in turn.

Pitfall 1: Going for any Resources, Instead of Focusing on Winning Ones with All Four Cornerstones

It is a fatal mistake to design a new offering that fails to use at least one resource with all four cornerstones. The only exception to this is the rare offering with a minimal payback period. That exceptional offering would only need a resource with two of them: distinctive and bargain.

The most prevalent example of forgetting winning resources can be described as me-tooism. We see firm X doing well with an innovative new tumble-drier, so we simply try to ape X and its drier. Suppose we manage to copy X exactly. In that case we may indeed force X to reduce its price and thus to reduce the value it generates. However, without a winning resource we ourselves shall be stuck with the same lower price, the same costs and the same lower returns. The offering is unlikely to generate value for us.

This is not to say that there is no way of prospering by competing closely with X. However, we shall only achieve that if we give customers better value than X, yet still have a positive NPV. We can either give them a more attractive drier or the same drier at a lower price and at a lower cost to ourselves. For that we need at least one winning resource, a resource which is distinctive, that is unique to ourselves, and a bargain, matchless and inseparable. We must transcend simple me-tooism. Just acquiring the brainpower to become another world-class firm of consultants or emulating best practice in managing relationships with customers for euro-denominated corporate bonds may seem like stretching objectives, but they are just another form of me-tooism. The effort must end in disappointment even if the objective is attained.

Another example of this pitfall is to go overboard on a resource which is a necessary condition of competing in (say) professional football, in this case a stadium. Without a stadium we could not compete. It is a *necessary* resource, but not a *sufficient* condition of creating value. For that we need one or more winning resources with all four cornerstones. Yet those managing a company which has just at great expense acquired a stadium will always be tempted to regard that necessary resource as a winning one. Yet all they have in fact obtained is a means of pursuing me-tooism!

The stadium is a fairly crude example of this error. However, we still perpetrate the same error if we go for more specialized or higher-quality resources, which yet lack one or more of the cornerstones. Suppose a consumer goods business becomes highly skilled at advertising, where previously it lagged behind. Or suppose a hospital acquires top-class medical staff, or an airline the very latest type of aircraft. In all these cases, if we are merely catching up with the competition, or if our new resource is easily replicated, we have not acquired a winning resource.

We can take this erroneous approach one step further to pure management resources. General Electric for many years had a well-known flair for structuring itself so as to get the best possible combination of central thrust with decentralized responsibility. In this it excelled. The resource was distinctive in that sense, but it was not of itself a winning one with all four cornerstones able to create any one winning offering. For example, such a resource does not ensure that any one offering adds value for the whole of its payback period, nor is it immune to replication, or to appropriation of its value by key employees or suppliers. It was again a valuable resource, but not a winning one. Those who hope that pure management resources can be winning ones are losing sight of the purpose of all this: to produce winning offerings. In any case less complex competitors, specialized in just a few interrelated offerings, might not need such a structure-building resource at all.

Failing to focus on *winning* resources amounts to ignoring the cornerstones altogether. It is also fatal, however, to rely on resources which have less than all four cornerstones. Below we illustrate how the absence of any one cornerstone can lead to failure. The strength of a chain is no greater than that of its weakest link.

Pitfall 2: Ignoring Bargain

When we have thought of a shining new offering, but need to find a winning resource to produce it, we tend to get carried away by the brilliance of the concept. So are we likely to worry whether the resource we have to buy will cost too much to leave us with any value from the new offering? Without enthusiasm there is no enterprise, but how well does enthusiasm mix with sordid calculation of what it costs to realize our dream? Energy and drive do not excuse us for falling into pitfalls like this one.

The big practical lesson here is that we must not enter into an auction to acquire a resource we want. If the market for the resource is sufficiently well oiled, an auction will ensue, and in that case the price we pay is very likely to transfer the whole value of the resource to the party that sells it to us. If this resource was the only way to produce our offering, we must abandon the offering. It will not build value for us.

Of course the value of the resource is not limited to what the resource can earn for us in *this* offering. If we can use it for *other* future offerings, the value to be achieved in them counts too. However, if we have not yet evaluated those other potential offerings, we must be cautious in what value we put on the contribution the resource will make to their success.

So the upshot from the bargain cornerstone is that either we must own and control the resource already or we must be able to obtain it in a sufficiently imperfect market to avoid an auction, and obtain it for a good deal less than its full value to us.

Pitfall 3: Ignoring the 'Distinctive' Cornerstone

The most brilliant resource will not generate value for us if others have it too, or a very similar one. If we could solve the problem of reducing the cost of seawater desalination to a competitive level, so as to tackle water shortages in many parts of the world, we might think it obvious that we must generate value. However, if that same know-how was available to competitors at the same cost, then we are far from likely to generate returns that beat our cost of capital. A resource must be diverse, and therefore company-specific to be a winning one.

The point is fundamental, but managers have been known to ignore it when a resource appears sufficiently glamorous. The stampede into investment banking skills in the 1980s and into dotcom skills in the late 1990s may have been examples of this. If others can build value in a glamorous new market, it does not follow that we can. We must do better than mere me-tooism.

Pitfall 4: Underestimating the Tendency for Encroachers to Muscle in on a Successful Offering: Hence the Need for Matchless and Inseparable

Planners of a promising new offering frequently underestimate the market tendency to encroach on the new offering. Such encroachment erodes the value expected by the planners. This tendency is really a more general description of some of the more specific errors that we are here discussing. Entrepreneurial genius is not always coupled with the wisdom of experience. It is natural to think of a brilliant new idea as a sure winner, rather than as a magnet to encroachers. Those who first marketed shaving oil as a substitute for shaving cream or gel may have assumed it would not be imitated; if they did, they surely miscalculated. This kind of approach comes close to being tactical rather than strategic.

Any evidently successful innovation will attract those who wish to get a piece of the action, unless that proves difficult or uneconomic. That occurs when the first mover has a necessary resource which is not easily open to imitation, bypass or enticement. The following example illustrates a failed enticement. A small engineering company made household goods of unusual and attractive designs in a small town. A competitor unsuccessfully advertised in the local paper for a designer of such household goods. The competitor was unaware that in this unusual case the gifted owner manager of the factory designed his own offerings, and was therefore an inseparable resource. However, the general point here is that we must be on the alert for encroachers. This is covered more specifically in pitfall 5.

Pitfall 5: Taking a Cavalier View of What Is Needed for Matchless or Inseparable

Pitfalls 4 and 5 have one main cause in common: a reluctance to face the need for value-building to be sustainable. A winning resource needs to be company-specific or distinctive not only now, but for the whole payback period.

A cavalier approach to this task can take two forms: underestimating the payback period or playing down the threat to sustainability. That threat can take the form of replication or bypassing by competitors, or of appropriation by other parties of the resource or its value. Pitfall 5 tempts us to ignore or underestimate these threats and the protective armour needed against them.

As an aside, we have noted the exceptional case of very short payback periods, where sustainability ceases to be a material problem. An example might be where a new washing detergent is merely marketed in a different colour like blue or green. However, such very rapid payback is rare, and should only be relied upon with great caution.

First, let us illustrate how easy and tempting it is to be cavalier about matchless. Suppose Seeforyourself Inc invented a relatively low-cost way for bedridden invalids to visually scan the shelves of their favourite supermarket with a simple hand-held device, to log their selections on a shopping list for delivery to their home and to arrange payment. Let us further suppose that Seeforyourself expected the technology to be fairly transparent to would-be encroachers, and therefore decided to charge only a moderate margin over cost. In that case it might be tempted to take an optimistic view of sales volumes and costs, and thus to rely on a hazardously short payback period immune to countermeasures by competitors. That optimism about the payback period is just as vulnerable as optimism about the price that can be charged. A feasibility study is vulnerable to *both* kinds of optimism.

It is equally tempting to be cavalier with inseparable. In the late 1980s, a foreign bank A in London found it hard to find a profitable activity in London's overcrowded banking scene. It decided that project finance was still a fairly rare skill. In classic me-tooist fashion bank A hired an expert from bank B, which excelled in project finance.

Bank A then actually landed one project in Europe. However, the expert was then poached by bank C before bank A had recovered the high investment in enticing him away from bank B.

If an attractive package was all that was needed to tempt the expert from B to A, then an even more attractive package could induce him either to move from A again or to hold A to ransom so as to appropriate his value to himself. A single expert is seldom an inseparable resource! Bank A's move failed some of the other cornerstones too.

All four cornerstones have to be met; any attempt to acquire resources that lack any of them is foolhardy.

Pitfall 6: Underestimating the Difficulty of Identifying One's Own Winning Resources

The pitfalls so far discussed amount to a defective understanding of the need for winning resources with all four cornerstones. This pitfall concerns strategists who respect the need for winning resources, who are even aware that the company is very likely to have some winning resources, but who now underestimate the difficulty of identifying them. The background is that winning resources by definition are unlikely to be easily visible or traded in the open market. Bargain carries its own special difficulty. The superior foresight needed for buying a winning resource as a bargain is rare indeed.

Our company is likely to have winning resources, because without them we are unlikely to have generated value in the past, and without generating value we are unlikely to have survived. The matchless cornerstone too makes it unlikely that our existing winning resources are easy to find. If we could easily find them, then our competitors too might find them reasonably identifiable, and then perhaps imitable. Obscurity is one of the best defences. Obscurity camouflaged the delivery drivers who generated customer loyalty, and who were nearly paid off because their own management was unaware that it was they who generated that loyalty.

We shall not design a winning offering if we cannot find at least one winning resource to produce it. We must either look for a winning resource among our existing resources or find one for which the market is so restricted that it meets all four cornerstones. We must face the fact that the search will be hard in either case, yet not impossible. It will be slightly easier in some rare cases with a very short payback period. It will also be easier for companies at the leading edge of technology: their challenge is to obtain and retain that lead.[1]

Pitfall 7: Ignoring the Opportunity Cost Principle

This pitfall is a temptation above all for entrepreneurial strategists more at home with marketing than with finance. When we have or acquire a valuable resource, our natural instinct is to use it, not to sell it. Yet we must sell it if that makes to company more valuable. In other words, if its worth to an outside party exceeds its NPV in our hands. The purpose of any business is to generate value, not to make widgets, not even the best ever widgets. Of course, if those widgets could generate more wealth than the price we can obtain for the relevant resource from another party, we should make the widgets. If not, we should sell the resource.

Resources that meet all four cornerstones will not often have an even greater disposal value, but in the few cases where they do, this pitfall can have serious consequences.

If the value of the resource is big enough, say a collection of town-centre supermarket sites, it could even make our company an attractive takeover target. If the potential buyer cannot buy the supermarket sites from us, and if that buyer can extract more value from the sites, it can afford to bid for our company, divest what it does not want of our assets and retain the cheaply acquired sites.

Summary

Winning resources may well be the most taxing topic in this book, but they are also one of the most rewarding topics. They are a condition of success which is often either overlooked or treated too lightly. This chapter has dealt with some of the pitfalls. However, winning resources are only one of the two elements in designing winning offerings.

The other element is a winning competitive position. The practical steps for combining both elements will be explored in Chapter 10.

Note

1. Prahalad, C.K. and Hamel, G. (1990). The core competence of the corporation. *Harvard Business Review*, May–June, 79–91.

10

Getting it together: The scissors process

Introduction

Our central message in this book is about the design of winning future offerings. A new offering must meet two main conditions: a winning competitive position, and the use of one or more winning resources. Neither on its own is enough to ensure financial success.[1] Winning competitive positions are discussed in Chapters 4–7, winning resources in Chapters 8–9. This chapter discusses the practical steps needed to combine these two requirements, so as to create a winning offering. Because the two efforts need to be indissolubly linked like the two blades of a pair of scissors, we call the combined process *the scissors process*. The name usefully reminds us that this process, first encountered in Chapter 1 and here illustrated in Figure 10.1, is at the cutting edge of strategizing.

The centrality of the *individual* offering is one of our recurring themes. Each offering has to be designed and evaluated in its own right. That is because each offering has a unique competitive position, not shared by any other offering of the same company: only an offering can be chosen by customers. That is an unavoidable fact of life on the customer or 'demand' side of the coin. On the 'supply' side, however, any viable offering is only too likely to share resources, winning or non-winning, with other offerings. Failure to share resources would reduce scale economies, and possibly make the other offerings uncompetitive. Hence *decisions* must often be taken about two or more

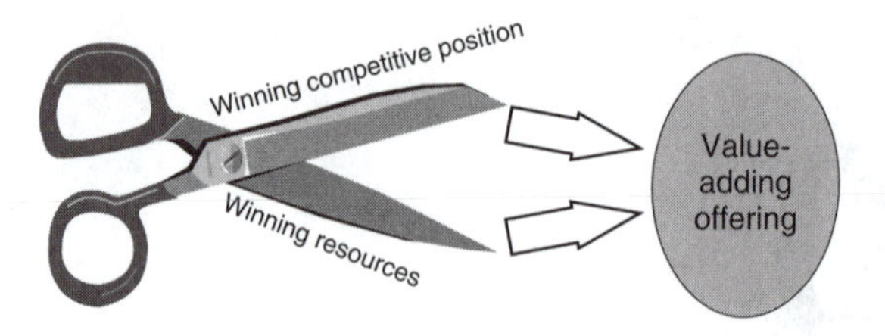

Figure 10.1 The scissors process

offerings together, but only after each offering and its competitive positioning has been *designed and evaluated* separately. This asymmetry between the demand and supply sides is inherent in the nature of business, and therefore also of competitive strategy. We shall be returning to this asymmetry in Chapter 11, which introduces corporate strategy.

Protecting Sustained Value Creation: Entrenched Positions with Customers

Encroachment – competitors coming in to imitate or replicate a profitable competitive position – is one of the most potent threats to value-building and to recovery of the cost of capital.

Protective armour against encroachment can be obtained on the supply side from matchless and inseparable resources. That was described in Chapter 8. However, protection can also in some cases be achieved on the demand side by the supplier becoming entrenched in some way with specific customers. Chapter 7 dealt with that. Where this occurs, competition is not just a matter of pure market processes, but subject to various types of barriers described in Chapters 3 and 7. Examples are as follows:

- Restriction of competition by interventionist governments.
- Discriminatory public procurement, for example in defence or public health services, where authorities use restricted lists of approved suppliers.

- Inconspicuousness, where offerings are bought by few customers. Competitors fail to move in due to sheer unawareness of the offering itself, or of its attraction to customers, or of its potential for wider customer groups, or of its high margins.

Resources to create such entrenchment barriers can occasionally be actively developed. Some of these can even turn out to be winning resources. The Kingdom of Rotten Bhanana, a small and corrupt developing country, may award lucrative contracts to favoured foreign suppliers. On the face of it this is a 'market' process of a certain kind. The one that bribes most becomes the favoured supplier. However, if X Inc's CEO's sister-in-law marries the King of Rotten Bhanana, this 'market' process may give way to a more secure favoured position for X. The entrenchment may be secure for a while. X does, however, face some potential threats. X's competitor Y may find another wife for the king, as bigamy is legal in Rotten Bhanana. Again, X may fall foul of competition or criminal law in its own country. Most likely of all, there may be a coup, followed by a change of regime in Rotten Bhanana.

Entrenchment can of course be a more normal and less dubious phenomenon. A flagship airline may induce its national airport authority to write the rules in such a way that it has a privileged position, with more landing 'slots' than its competitors. Similarly, UK broadcasters by auction have won a limited number of commercial TV franchises from the broadcasting authorities. The winners have won tenure for a stated number of years. That tenure might in some cases be a winning resource, if it has all four cornerstones.

Quite commonly, however, such rules are written differently. The government may have an arbitrary power to extend or modify a list of approved suppliers at will. Here there may still be a potential winning resource, capable of ensuring recovery of the cost of capital. Our company may, for example, have an informal understanding that it can count on remaining on the approved list. It all depends on how the authority exercises and communicates its power to write and operate the rules. The essence of this potential winning resource in these, not very common cases, is the company's ability to *rely upon*, rather than *control* its privileged tenure. This informal, non-legal tenure is less robust than the typical, physically or legally controlled winning resource. It may nevertheless meet the cornerstones if the company is satisfied that it can see off any attempts to oust or erode its favoured position during the payback period. The whole issue may even be insignificant if the offering has a short payback period, as discussed in Chapters 8 and 9. We need, however, to be very clear that this is relatively light armour, resting on confidence without control.

The *inconspicuous offering* is a different and interesting case. The company's superior awareness of the favourable competitive position is clearly a resource. The environmental opaqueness of the opportunity is just a market condition. We must judge how reliable this opaqueness is over the payback period. The threats must be assessed. They are usually outside the company's control. For example, where a niche offering is simply not widely known, customers might get enthusiastic and broadcast its existence. The strategy should go ahead only if the company is confident that it could, if need be, see off all success-aping attempts for the whole payback period. If yes, and if all four cornerstones are in place, we have a winning resource. But all that is a long shot.

The issue of sustained value-building can be summed up as follows:

- In the majority of cases sustainability is safeguarded on the supply side by winning resources, sometimes for a succession of serially innovative offerings. Winning resources have degrees of robustness.
- Sustainability is quite commonly protected on the demand side by entrenched positions. Ideally the company has some control over these barriers, but something short of control is sometimes adequate where the seller has grounds for confidence that an entrenched position will outlast the payback period. Here the company's ability to count on that entrenchment can constitute a winning resource.

Finding and Harnessing Winning Resources

We here set out the entire process of designing a winning new offering, bringing together the achievement of a winning competitive position with the deployment of one or more winning resources. One of the major difficulties is that of identifying our winning resources. We saw in Chapter 8, when describing the bargain cornerstone, that winning resources are seldom acquired by superior foresight. They are usually already owned and controlled, and sometimes acquired by luck.

Winning resources are in many cases (a) already owned, (b) originally acquired or developed for some other purpose and (c) inconspicuous. These features help to meet one or more of the cornerstones. However, they make our winning resources hard to find not just for others, but also for ourselves. They are *meant* to be hard to find! Some degree of concealment from ourselves is the price of keeping others guessing.

Resources are of course of many kinds. They can be tangible or intangible. They can be real estate, plant and machinery, inventory, scientific knowledge, patents, know-how, other individual or collective human skills, operating routines and so on. Moreover, knowledge resources can be held at the corporate centre, further down the line or at the coalface.

We can look for winning resources by searching in all these categories or places. However, the cornerstones are much more likely to be met by one narrow category of resources: collective skills and routines. Teams of people develop joint skills and procedures, often without explicit awareness. These resources are the hardest for outsiders to spot, the hardest for others to copy, poach or appropriate, and the most likely to be bargains. The company has better control of them.

Team skills and routines are not of course the only kind of winning resources. We have several times referred to unique sites or physical facilities. For example, a site may have been acquired for a petrol station, yet now become much more valuable for a new supermarket. However, that asset is unlikely to be completely hidden from outsiders. Yes, we can refuse to sell that site, but the opportunity to refuse a sale may indicate that the resource is more valuable to others. If so, we must sell it and realize the higher price. Moreover, as we have seen, if the site accounts for a significant part of the value of our company, we may attract a hostile takeover bid from a predator whose main purpose is to get hold of the site. Such real estate is also in many cases capable of close substitution. Again, there are highly distinctive knowledge assets held by individual employees, but those individuals are vulnerable to poaching or able to appropriate the value of the resource for themselves. All this reinforces the logic of the predominance among winning resources of collective skills and routines. They are a promising area of search.

Nevertheless, this sounds like bad news. If winning resources are typically obscure and hard to pinpoint, then how *can* we identify our winning resources? The best method by far is to analyse our company's past successes, and to search for the secret of their success. There is a strong presumption that a winning resource was involved. That is the best way to look for winning resources already owned. This is no coincidence. Success comes from exploiting one's own company's points of excellence.

This avenue of search is promising, as we said, because there is a good chance that our winning resources are already in our possession and have been winners before. On the other hand we may well possess potential winners now, which were not winning resources previously. We must not restrict our search to past winners. Finding winning resources will never be easy, nor is there a single way to achieve that task, but the suggestions made here should be of some help.

Where to Begin: with the Competitive Position or with the Winning Resource?

If we are looking for a new offering, we have the twin tasks of looking for a winning competitive position and at least one winning resource. These are the twin blades of the scissors, as in Figure 10.1.

However, which blade should we search first? On which side should we start, on the supply side or on the demand side? We might start on the demand side and look for a winning competitive position, very attractive to customers and not too vulnerable to attack from competitors. We might hope to have either the lowest unit costs for a commodity-buy or a differentiated offering with a value-building combination of margin and volume. Having identified our potentially winning position, we might then look for a winning resource to make that position ours, and to fortify it against encroachers.

The other option is to look on the supply side for one or more winning resources, and then for a winning competitive position in which those specific resources will give us competitive advantage, which for our purposes means value sustained until the cumulative value built by the offering turns positive.

However, do we always need to make a choice between tackling the demand or the supply side first?

Wide Choice or Narrow?

When we set out to design a new offering, are we scouring the whole world for ideas? Should our CEO sit down with a blank sheet, and ask whether to market nuclear power stations, or fruit juices, or copying machines or new drawing software? This question is a central issue of corporate strategy and will be pursued in depth in Chapter 12. However, a brief view needs to be taken here.

What we might in fact be exploring may be influenced by whether ours is an existing business or a new one. In an existing business we might probably think in incremental terms. We think about modifying existing offerings, exploring similar market areas in which we have some feel for the interplay of customers and competitors, and exploiting or leveraging our existing skills and other resources. Wal-Mart would probably not consider building a bridge from Sicily to the Italian mainland, and Halliburton might not perhaps be interested in opening a beauty salon. In any case, the choice may also be narrowed if the company has defined and declared its scope, that is what businesses it is in. This concept of the company's scope is discussed in Chapter 12.

How about a new business? A new entrepreneur may have no previous track record in business. Nevertheless, she might aim at serving the kind of market which she already understands, and at using a winning resource which she personally believes she has. If she has a brilliant idea about designing a new and better yacht, that may be because she has experience of sailing one, and knows something about the construction of boats. She might not, however, wish to consider the alternative of going into refuse collection or pharmaceutical research. She too therefore does not start with a blank sheet, but with a narrower set of more promising options. In a narrow field in which we have some superior expertise, we may well start with some grasp both of winning competitive positions and of the kind of resources that might turn out to be winners for our company.

To sum this up, commonsense will prompt us to restrict our choices to a relatively narrow front. Our company is likely to think about a customer market or segment that is not wholly outside its experience, and of an offering which enables it to exploit its existing strengths: to aim at excelling in target arenas. That is precisely what the scissors approach does.

How to Start the Scissors Process

We were debating on which side to start. Should we look for a winning competitive position first, or for winning resources first? To answer this, it is useful to consider three different scenarios:

1. the company knows where it excels;
2. the market area and the resources needed in it have natural links; and
3. other situations.

The company knows where it excels

If we are looking for a new offering in a market area close to where we have had a previous winner, then the odds are that the previous and the new winner will use either the same winning resources or very similar ones. We may not know what those winning resources were, but the best clue is hidden in the success of the previous winner. It pays to search for an explanation of its success. So our effective starting-point is not the competitive position, nor the resource, but the previous successful offering.

Similarly, if a new entrepreneur knows what they are good at, it is very likely that they have a very good idea why a certain market area will benefit from whatever special skill they know they have. Their starting-point too is neither the competitive position nor the resource, but their sense of where they excel on *both* fronts. Of course, as a new entrepreneur they may not have to look for *collective* skills. At this stage they are often on their own, and they themselves are not separable! It is a different matter if they depend on an irreplaceable supplier, subcontractor, partner or employee.

Of course, as a business matures, it may well gain extra and different competences. If it starts out with excellence in marketing confectionery, it may after some years become good at designing some stage in the production process, such as quality control or chocolate coating or efficient distribution channels. At that point it may have developed a very different winning resource, which it can add to its exploitable opportunities.

The market area and the resources needed in it have natural links

A relatively narrow field of search applies also where we do not start with our own field of excellence, but where the market area and the resource have natural links. Pharmaceutical manufacture goes hand in hand with research laboratories, catering goes with food purchasing expertise. Teams with that skill might be less interested in offering IT consultancy. Natural links are very common. The winning skills for retailing are not very similar to those for drilling for oil. Nor is there any close commonality between those needed in retail banking and running a convenience store. To some extent the competitive position and the resource select each other. That simplifies the search. Neither search begins with a blank sheet: it can be quite narrowly restricted, to a more manageable range of possibilities.

Other situations

There are other cases where the possibilities are less restricted, or where any links between the market area and the resource are less evident. Examples might be where one or the other is relatively new and unfamiliar. In 2005, Avon was considering employing Avon Ladies to sell financial products in addition to cosmetics.[2] We have already seen that obscurity is a useful feature of winning resources, but it can also apply to market areas, where significant and not widely understood changes are taking place in the attitudes and preferences of customers. Early in the twenty-first century, fast foods are changing rapidly in response to obesity fears. Even here the lists of possible winning resources may not be as wide open as might be thought.

There are those who suggest a *general* rule that the process should start with winning resources. One suggested reason is that there are fewer such resources than possible competitive positions. Another is that the company's resources are a more important constraint, because companies should 'stick to the knitting'. That last thought may inadequately distinguish between winning and other resources. It should be remembered that winning resources are often hard to discover, and above all that the same winning resource does not necessarily benefit all or even many offerings. Still more importantly, that view may overestimate the extent to which success is dependent on winning resources rather than an appreciation of customer preferences. These can move independently of the actions of suppliers, as for example when fur coats went out of fashion. Moreover, some business leaders are better at marketing than at controlling their own operations, and therefore better at finding profitable market opportunities. Once such an opportunity has been identified, a more specific search for a winning resource may then be easier.

The choice is easier for technological leaders with the skill of remaining ahead in their technologies. They may well do best to keep looking for new applications for their leading edge excellence. However, their case is not nearly as common as is sometimes tacitly assumed.

The conclusion is that there is no *general* rule that either the market area or the resource is the better starting-point. Even in this third category it is best to be pragmatic, to treat each choice as a separate challenge, and to look here too for shortcuts to limit the field of search in the light of the facts.

Testing for Robustness

Each new offering needs a test for robustness. Robustness is akin to a fail-safe concept. The new offering must earn its cost of capital even in adverse circumstances. Examples are as follows:

- worse than assumed *general* conditions, such as a recession in the world or domestic economy;
- adverse changes in the preferences of customers, such as changing fashions;
- new offerings developed by competitors during the pre-launch gestation period of our offering; and finally
- countermeasures by competitors after the successful launch of our new offering; examples would be price reductions to protect their market shares, or imitations of our offering.

Sensitivity analysis should be employed for this testing process. We shall return to the 'robust' concept in Chapter 13.

Steps of the Scissors Process: Starting with Resources

Finally, we list the practical sequence of steps in the scissors process. First, we assume that we have chosen to begin with the resource side, perhaps because we are confident that we know the actual or potential winning resources for the task in hand. We further assume that we have a narrow range of possible offerings in mind.

1. Ascertain the list of actual or potential winning resources.
2. Outline the market areas where these resources can create winning offerings.
3. Scan those promising market areas for gaps or niches in which our company may have exceptional opportunities to excel profitably. The gap might consist either of future offerings at a suitable and sustainable distance from likely future substitutes or of future commodity-buys for which our company has a sustainable cost advantage.
4. Rank potential offerings by NPV. Use normal project evaluation techniques for this, taking care to evaluate the NPV of each offering in terms of its impact on the company or group of companies as a whole.
5. Test the most promising ones for threats, with a sensitivity analysis. Among other things, this requires a search of competitors with imitating or bypassing resources.
6. Choose the best sufficiently robust offering. The offering and its winning resources must be robust enough to weather adverse competitive or other developments until the cost of capital has been recovered.

Steps of the Scissors Process: Starting with Competitive Positions

Alternatively, assume that we have reason to begin with the demand side, that is with promising competitive positions:

1. Look for promising competitive positions with profitable gaps for either differentiated or cheaper offerings.

2. Look at each promising competitive position and see whether we are likely to have a winning resource to exploit it. Remember that the resource may operate at any point of the value chain. Bear in mind that our past successes are a promising clue to winning resources of which we may not yet be aware.
3. List candidate offerings with the potential for sustainable success.
4. Rank the offerings by NPV.
5. Test the most promising ones for threats, with a sensitivity analysis.
6. Choose the best sufficiently robust offering.

Summary of the Scissors Process

The scissors process describes the process of choosing a new offering. It brings together the two blades of the scissors, winning resources and winning competitive position. Either blade might be the starting-point in the choice process, depending on the company, on the skills of the strategist and on the nature of the options open to us. In any case the two blades tend to get intertwined in the process. Ideally the whole search is conducted over a well chosen area, narrow enough to exclude options outside the company's field of excellence, but wide enough to include new opportunities that might be within its scope in a changing world.

A Look Back at Competitive Strategy

This completes Part 3 and our look at the issues of competitive strategy. Each new offering needs a strategy. A new offering must have a winning competitive position and use one or more winning resources. These are the two blades of the scissors, and neither blade can do the job on its own.

A winning competitive position is one which enables the offering to have a positive NPV through either

- differentiation;
- dependable favourable entry barriers (Chapter 7); or
- a sustainable advantage in unit costs.

A winning resource has the four cornerstones. It must be distinctive, a bargain, matchless and inseparable.

We now leave the field of competitive strategy and in Part 4 turn to corporate strategy, which manages the company's collection of winning offerings.

Notes

1. Strategy literature has long argued for matching the demand-side and the supply-side. See Priem, R.L. and Butler, J.E. (2001). Is the resource-based 'view' a useful perspective for strategic management research? *Academy of Management Review*, **26**(1), 22–40. Our approach follows in this tradition. Our focus is however on the offering rather than any other unit.
2. Avon calling: how's your insurance? *The Business*, 20/21 February 2005, p. 13.

PART 4

Corporate Strategy: Managing the Collection of Offerings

Parts 2 and 3 have set out a framework for designing individual new offerings. The focus has been on decisions about future positions in customer markets, decisions which have to be proposed by managers close enough to those markets. The decisions can nevertheless affect other parts of the company, and need approval from the CEO.

In Part 4, we address the task of building value by managing a company's *collection* of offerings. This is *corporate* strategy, and is a task for top management. Chapter 11 describes the nature and task of corporate strategy and its need to pursue financial value. Chapter 12 deals with the vital issue of relatedness. It suggests that offerings should be related to the rest of the company, and clarifies what precisely makes an offering 'related'. Chapter 13 sets out the other criteria of value creation that should be applied to every decision to add, retain or divest an offering.

The timely divestment of offerings that have ceased to build value is one of the greatest but widely neglected contributions that corporate strategy can make to a company's success.

11

Corporate strategy: Its nature and aim

Introduction

Chapter 2 suggested that all business strategy aims to create long-term value for the investors in the business. Chapters 4–10 discussed *competitive strategy*, which in this book is seen as the design of a single new offering that will create value. This chapter switches the reader's attention from the single new offering to the totality of the company's collection of offerings. *Corporate strategy* manages that totality.

It is sometimes said that equity investors can only react to news about a company by taking a buy, hold or sell decision. Similarly corporate strategy makes decisions

- to add offerings to the collection, that is to 'diversify';
- to retain offerings in the collection; or
- to divest offerings.

Corporate strategy, like competitive strategy in this book, needs to evaluate and review individual offerings, but its *decisions* often have to cover more than one offering. For although each offering has a unique competitive position vis-à-vis customers and competitors, it nevertheless normally shares costs, resources and facilities with other offerings. On the demand or customer side each offering has to be analysed individually, whereas on the supply side several offerings

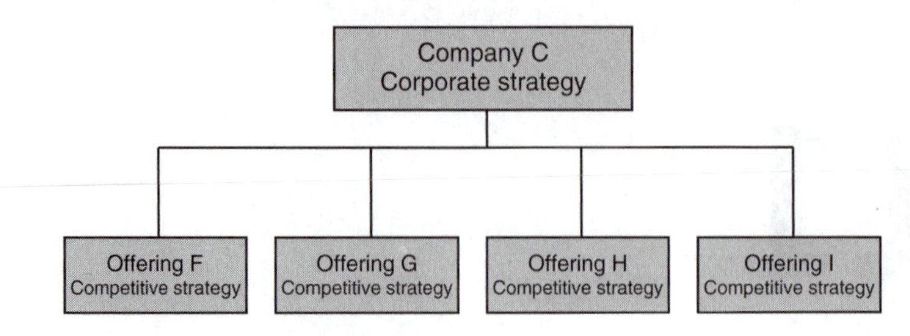

Figure 11.1 Company and offerings

tend to need collective attention. This asymmetry between the two sides is inherent in the nature of business, and a major fact of business.

Figure 11.1 illustrates the respective tasks of competitive and corporate strategy.

Many people, like this book, see corporate strategy as deciding what activities the company should continue, add or drop. However, the activities are usually taken to be profit centres, business units or divisions, whereas in this book they are offerings.[1] We treat the offering as the critical strategic unit because it is only offerings that customers choose and it is their choices that determine a company's success or failure.

The tasks of corporate strategy consist of:

a. Constantly monitoring whether the composition of the collection of offerings can be made more valuable.
b. Evaluating each proposal for a new offering, to see if it would add value to the collection as a whole. How would it affect other offerings in that collection?
c. Reviewing all existing offerings to see whether any of them have ceased to generate value. Is the company better off *today* if it retains a specific offering P or not?

During much of the twentieth century too many corporate strategies were seen to fail.[2] There was an excessive desire to expand companies into too many offerings, fed by some unhelpful doctrines and by neglect of the extra costs of diversified operation. Our framework for corporate strategy suggests some strong countermeasures against these tendencies.

The view of corporate strategy taken here may at first sight appear very restrictive, and even anti-entrepreneurial. That reaction is partly a misunderstanding. Our approach is selective, not restrictive. We do encourage growth and diversification, but only the sort that generates financial value. Hostility to our approach is also partly due to two other factors. The first is that practical strategists do not always have a perfect grasp of the financial criteria of success and survival. The second is the widespread worship of size. These two issues have been covered in Chapter 2. The fact is that in the modern world small, narrowly focused companies often perform better than large, complex ones. On the other hand many over-diversified companies, for example those called 'conglomerates', fail to earn their cost of capital and end in failure.[3]

It may be thought that this experience is the fault not of poor performance by highly diversified companies, but by the bias of equity markets against wide ranges of offerings leading them to raise the cost of capital of those conglomerates. In fact the downgrading of conglomerates by equity markets was not a cause, but a consequence of poor performance confirmed by research.

Hence our main reason for advocating a relatively selective view of corporate strategy is the poor record of diversification strategies since (say) 1950. Too many of them have failed.

Companies have been far too gung-ho and unselective about expanding into new offerings. Equally, they have been too protective and timid about pruning their collections. Every offering ultimately has its sell-by date, when it ceases to add value to its present owner. Some never did fit in the first place. Even more opportunities tend to get missed by hanging on to existing offerings than by failing to add value-building new ones. We know of a small business whose owner even in 1990 could not accept that animal fur coats had lost their market. Many managers hold on to what they believe is their company's core business long after it has become an incurable loss-maker. 'Core' businesses are more often than not obsolete. If so, they should be got rid of. Even core skills have to be shed if they can no longer be used to serve profitable customers. The purpose of corporate strategy is to ensure that *all* parts of the company build value for it, irrespective of whether they are 'core' or otherwise.

To sum this up, some managers will resist the selective and anti-size approach of this book. This is understandable because managers as a group have for decades been conditioned to accept the contrary rush for size. That philosophy has had a very poor track record, and has been heavily criticized by Michael Porter and many others since 1980.[4]

Some Still Believe in Conglomerates: The Case of Hewlett-Packard

Business opinion and stock market sentiment has since then turned against large conglomerates. There is, however, still some resistance. Carly Fiorina became CEO of Hewlett-Packard (HP) in 1999. At that time, as reported by the *Financial Times*,[5] HP consisted of 87 separate and largely self-contained business units. She not only consolidated and integrated them into a more monolithic corporate structure, but also implemented the acquisition of Compaq, taking HP into yet more electronic offerings and markets. All this was against the received wisdom. However, she strengthened the performance of this conglomerate by cutting out duplicated costs and achieving substantial savings in centralized procurement costs. Some of HP's divisions were turned round from loss to profit. Nevertheless, the *Financial Times* said in October 2004, 'At $56bn HP is worth only about as much as its successful printer business would be if it was a stand-alone company.' Ms Fiorina's response to her critics was, 'This is a networked, integrated company for a broad, networked world.' 'The full portfolio matters more than ever. The big will get bigger and the small will get smaller.' This was a defiant reassertion of an old and widely discredited philosophy, not shared by this book. On 10 February 2005, Ms Fiorina resigned as CEO of HP. The policy to acquire Compaq had been backed by a less than united HP board,[6] but she became its determined implementer and spokesperson. When the board saw the need to acknowledge the adverse reaction of the stock market, she remained committed. A good strategy does not work without good implementation, but good implementation is not enough to make a bad strategy work. Sadly, what is not worth doing at all is also not worth doing well.

Others Do Not: Peninsular & Orient Steam Navigation Company

Robert Woods took over as CEO of Peninsular & Orient Steam Navigation Company (P&O) in January 2004. The P&O had a long history in the shipping industry. However, at the beginning of December 2003 its main activities were its ferry division, a container port division, a property division, a cold logistics division, which transported refrigerated goods and a 50 per cent holding in its joint venture P&O Nedlloyd, and another 50 per cent holding in Associated Bulk Carriers, as well as an Australian resorts business. Its shipping activities consisted mainly of cross-Channel ferries, which encountered strong competition from low-cost airlines and the Channel Tunnel. The *Financial Times* of 2 November 2004[7] showed that of these disparate businesses the container port activity was by far the most profitable. In 2003, it had earned three-fourth of P&O's operating profit on less than one-fourth of its turnover. The ferries had made a loss.

In December 2003, the holding in Associated Bulk Carriers was sold. By the time of the article in the *Financial Times*, Robert Woods had sold the Australian resorts business and half of P&O's holding in P&O Nedlloyd, and had committed P&O to the sale of its property portfolio. The plan for the ferries was to continue the programme of restructuring and general efficiency improvements. On completion of that programme a decision was to be taken about the future of the ferries.

The corporate strategy was clearly to restrict P&O to what it did best, the container port business, which was not only profitable but had a good growth potential. It changed the fortunes of the company and its shareholders. In November 2005, P&O received a takeover bid from Dubai Ports World (DPW) which after being recommended by the board was topped by a bid from Singapore's PSA International. In February 2006, shareholders voted in favour of an increased offer from DPW.

The Business[8] commenting on the preliminary takeover approach by DPW said the following:

> Whatever the final outcome of last week's tentative approach to P&O, it is likely to be seen as a tribute to the success of the company's

> recent restructuring . . . Until six years ago, P&O was an unfocused conglomerate with interests ranging from housebuilding to cruises. The overhaul that started in 1999 . . . set P&O on its current course.

It is this kind of corporate strategy that this book is advocating.

The Case of AT&T

In the first issue of *The McKinsey Quarterly* of 1999 in an article entitled 'Breaking Up', Patricia Anslinger and colleagues give a telling example of the phenomenon:[9]

> AT&T's 1996 ownership restructuring provides a striking example. Before the company announced that it would spin off Lucent Technologies and NCR, its market value was just $75 billion. Little more than a year later, in January 1998, the separately trading AT&T, Lucent, and NCR had a combined market capitalization of $159 billion.

Corporate Strategy Too Needs to Target Profitable Customers

A key focus in this book is on how our customers perceive us as their supplier. The experience of supermarkets, especially Wal-Mart, is that an expansion of their range will make them more successful. However, that is because most customers treat the supermarket itself with its broad range as a single offering, competing against rival supermarkets. That does not appear to be how customers see a company like HP which supplies both PCs and printers. They predominantly compare PCs with other PCs and printers with other printers. HP is not a single offering: it markets many separate offerings. This, in 2005, was equally true of a retailer like Boots in the United Kingdom.

We here develop some further arguments against the old pursuit of size for its own sake. It is to be hoped that the combined weight of these arguments will persuade managers to concentrate on skills and markets in which they excel and are able to build value.

The main issues reviewed in this and the next two chapters are as follows:

a. corporate strategy's objective of creating value, discussed in this chapter;

b. relatedness between offerings, and why this is an essential condition of successful diversification in Chapter 12; and
c. the other criteria of successful diversification, that is the better-off test and three filters, in Chapter 13.

Chapter 15 reviews the process of managing the collection and allocating resources.

Mergers, Acquisitions and Disposals, and Internal Additions of Offerings

The vast majority of additions and divestments of offerings occur by internal action within a company. The company replaces an offering or starts one up or discontinues an existing one.

We have already seen in Chapter 3 – under the heading *Competitive positions are not immortal* – that an offering is new whenever it occupies a new competitive position. One example is where it has been repositioned by the company.

Other transactions occur quietly between companies selling one or more offerings to each other. Thus BZW (Barclays Bank's investment bank subsidiary) sold its equity business to CSFB in 1997. Similarly, BMW sold the Rover business with the exception of the Mini in a management buy-out in 2000. The multitude of small transactions is of little public interest. There is more interest in wholesale transfers of entire profit centres or even divisions between companies. What receive most publicity, however, are mergers and takeovers, where independent companies are acquired by other companies. These takeovers can be friendly or hostile. They are typically transacted in stock markets under rules set by each such market and by corporate law. That takeover market is sometimes called the 'market in corporate control'.[10] Its main function is to ensure that underexploited assets come to be owned by companies able to extract better value from them. The market in corporate control also acts as a discipline on ineffective managements, transferring control of underperforming assets to more effective managers.

Two easily disregarded aspects of this topic need to be stressed:

1. The predominance in corporate strategy of internal and private transactions.
2. Where whole companies, divisions or other larger units change hands, and the acquirer obtains some offerings which do, and others which do not, build value for it, the latter should of course be redivested as soon as possible.

The Distinguishing Tasks and Skills of Corporate Strategy

One major task of corporate strategy overlaps with the task of competitive strategy: the addition of new offerings to the collection. Even here, however, there is a difference. A new offering is usually designed and proposed by managers or sponsors (see Chapter 14) close to the intended customers. That is the task of competitive strategy. The manager or sponsor concerned needs to consider other offerings affected by the proposed new offering, if it depends on resources used by those other offerings, or if it is likely to reduce or increase sales of those other offerings. The proposal to add the new offering then has to be approved by the CEO. The CEO's function is to apply an even wider yardstick, assessing the impact of the new offering on the company and its collection as a whole, including offerings of which the sponsor may not be aware. That process belongs to corporate strategy.

If an offering is aimed at sales to say the People's Republic of China, it may affect the prospects of other offerings in that country, even if they are marketed by otherwise unrelated parts of the company. A non-political example is Ford making its Aston Martin subsidiary abandon parts of its collection of clothing and accessories which were felt to be too risqué.[11]

The other big task of corporate strategy is the constant review of the whole collection and the search for offerings that need to be divested, if they no longer generate financial value. This task is very different from that of competitive strategy:

- Whereas the design of new offerings is often a one-off process, review of the collection is a continuous task.

- Corporate strategy continues to review offerings at later, often much later stages, in their lives. Competitive strategy analyses a given offering before conception, before the decision to commit to that project. By the time corporate strategy reviews that offering at later stages, it has a track record. The remaining life of the offering is that much shorter, and the uncertainties are that much less.
- Competitive strategy's task is creative and entrepreneurial. Corporate strategy's task is more coldly analytical. It checks whether the offering has a positive value at the time of review. However, its potential for improving the company's performance is enormous. Perfection would be to divest – that is to sell or terminate – each offering at the exact point in time where it ceases to build value and before it starts losing value for the company. The closer the company gets to this ideal, the more value destruction it prevents. The company that gets close to it will perform substantially better than most companies. Most companies continue offerings well into the period of value destruction.

This distinctive task of looking for offerings to divest tends to repel managers. It admittedly lacks glamour. Nevertheless, its rewards can be mouth-watering![12]

Illustration: Worthwhile Hotels

We can illustrate the need to focus on value with Worthwhile Hotels, an imaginary chain of three-star hotels listed on the London Stock Exchange. Out of the blue its Chairman received by telephone an offer of £7 million from a well-known US casino owner and property tycoon for the Bournemouth Worthwhile Hotel. The Chairman of Worthwhile, unused to the accent, misheard the figure and asked the tycoon to confirm that it was £10 million. That confirmation was duly given. The Worthwhile board had just valued the Bournemouth hotel at an NPV of £3 million as a hotel, and had no reason to think it had a greater disposal value. Unknown to the Worthwhile directors, the US tycoon, who was in the gaming business, had reason to believe that he could obtain a licence to open a casino.

Worthwhile had no opportunity to reinvest the £10 million proceeds of such a sale in another hotel or other value-building asset. It would therefore have to return the proceeds to shareholders as a special dividend. If so, the group might lose its status as a member of the FTSE 250 index. That would marginally raise Worthwhile's cost of capital. However, that burden would represent only a fraction of the £7 million value gain from selling to the US tycoon for £10 million. The Chairman and his board could not afford to turn down the offer. It made the company smaller in sales, in physical units, in market share and even in market capitalization, but it boosted the company's financial value.

The Payback Period: Characteristic Biography of a Value-Building Offering

Figure 11.2 (which we have already encountered in Chapter 2 as Figure 2.1) illustrates how a typical offering takes time to get the point where it builds value. Value is at first negative during the investment phase, and turns positive when the offering begins to produce positive cash flows. The illustration shows value created month-by-month, not

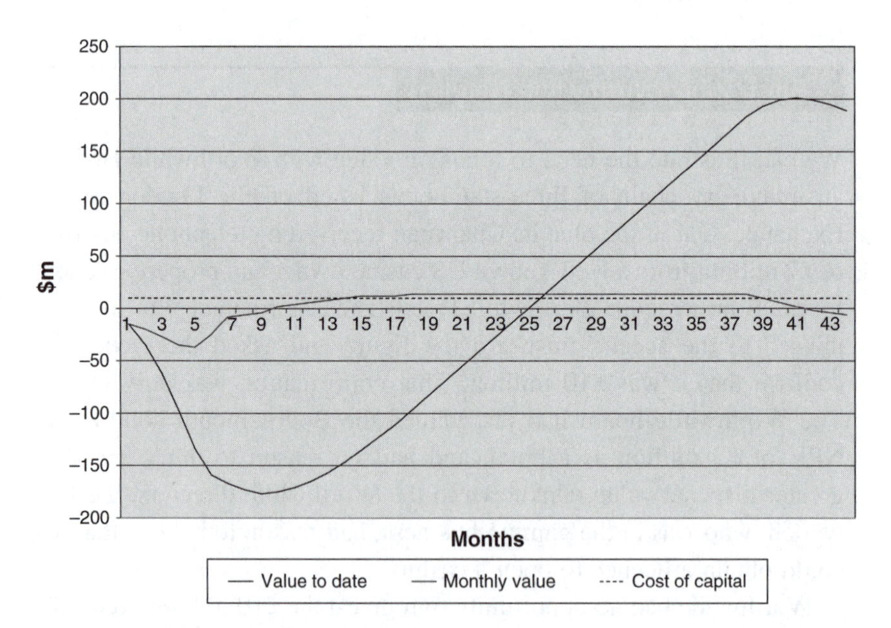

Figure 11.2 Value building by offering

net *present* value at a single point in time. The cost of capital is therefore treated as dollar cost, not as a discount factor.

The emphasis here is on the point at which the offering will ultimately cease to build value. Here the monthly value turns negative and the cumulative value-to-date peaks and then turns down. In Figure 11.2, this occurs in month 41. That is the best time to divest the offering.

Conflicts of Interest About the Objective of Financial Value

Chapter 2 reviewed rival objectives to the creation of financial value. These were risk diversification, size and the stakeholder view. In the context of corporate strategy top managers have been known to have personal interests which conflict with the value objective, and therefore to prefer one or another rival objective.

Briefly, the conflicting interests concern:

- *Status and remuneration*: A top manager's status and remuneration tends to increase with the size of the company and therefore decline with any reduction in that size.[13] This may predispose such a manager against any divestments that might improve the company's financial value, but reduce its size. Similarly it might prejudice her in favour of any acquisition or project that might improve the company's size, but not its value.
- *Job security*: Top managers generally have poor job security. If the stock market sees the company's shares performing badly, sentiment easily becomes unfavourable to the CEO. The Lex column in the *Financial Times*[14] of 3/4 September 2005 said, 'annual CEO turnover is now 12 per cent in the US and 17 per cent in Europe'.
- Preoccupation with this lack of job security can motivate CEOs to work against the value objective in three ways:
  - They may favour objectives like risk diversification or even the stakeholder view. If they could persuade the market of either of these, their performance would become less measurable and hence less vulnerable to criticism.
  - The lack of job security can predispose CEOs to reject takeover bids that add value for investors. A takeover bid for the company may represent a clear value gain for the shareholders, yet

inevitably result in the CEO losing his or her job. In that situation the CEO's clear duty is to recommend the bid, but his or her personal incentive is to resist.
- The CEOs might in the interests of their own job security shun projects with high risks and commensurately high prospective returns. If they single-mindedly pursued the value objective, they would go for such projects.

These conflicts of interest are real. They have made it harder to find good top managers. However, the answer to that is not for companies to adopt objectives other than value. It is much better to aim at remuneration packages for CEOs which include golden parachutes. Ideally, such parachutes are designed neither to overcompensate nor to undercompensate for loss of office, and to encourage good entrepreneurial performance.

Returning Capital to Owners

The preoccupation of top managers with size manifests itself in a very special way when a company's main business is coming to an end. The reason could, for example, be technological change. The switch over to digital cameras has sharply reduced the demand for film processors. Another reason is shifts in customer markets. A number of specialized retail businesses like health food stores and even liquor stores have been killed by the entry of supermarkets. Developments like these can leave the old company without winning resources and without areas where the top managers' skills continue to have a competitive advantage.

When a company can no longer employ some or even all its assets as value-builders, then those assets need to be realized, and the cash returned to owners. This is often the unwelcome, but inexorable end of a mature business which no longer has resources capable of generating value. No business has a permanent life, as is suggested by the fact that since the launch of the FTSE 100 index in 1984, only 42 of the original 100 were still on the index by April 2005.[15]

In such circumstances the proper course is voluntary liquidation, but that proper step rarely occurs.[16] Managers have a natural and emotive reluctance to terminate their own and their fellow employees' jobs. What they in fact resist is the recognition that the business is already terminally ill. If it were not, there would be no need to liquidate. In fact, their personal employment prospects outside their present business might well be better if they were seen to face the facts, and to sail the ship into the scrap yard before it sinks.

That reluctance is nowadays strangely encouraged by the stakeholder view. One of its components sees the company as partly the property of its employees, and sees the purpose of the company as providing stable employment. The stakeholder view and its difficulties are discussed in Chapter 2.

Corporate Strategy is a Task for Top Management

In the smallest or simplest business a single owner/manager takes all the important decisions. Complex businesses have levels of management, such as parent companies and subsidiaries, divisions and other profit centres. In such complex companies corporate strategy is the function of the top managers in the parent company, because only they have an overview over the whole of the company's collection of offerings. They alone can therefore assess whether offering X makes that collection more valuable.

However, that rule concerns just *decisions* or final approvals. Proposals for adding or divesting offerings often or even normally come from lower-level managers, including sponsors discussed in Chapter 14, closer to the offerings. They will do all the hard work of analysing each proposal and completing a viability study. All this leaves top management with the inalienable functions of

- assessing the impact of any proposal on the collection of all offerings, that is on the whole company, and
- monitoring the collection as a whole for weaknesses or possible improvements: a weeding function.

The functions of these respective sets of managers are discussed in Part 5 in Chapters 14 and 15.

Diversification

'Diversification' is a word often used by managers and others as a central issue of corporate strategy. Unfortunately, its special meaning in this context is not always well understood, because in common parlance it is taken to mean the addition of *diverse*, that is unrelated offerings or activities. Instead, it is in corporate strategy used to refer to the addition of *any* new activities, or in this book of *any* new offerings, related or unrelated to the existing collection.[17] That issue of related or unrelated has been the subject of a protracted debate:

- *Related* diversification adds offerings which have something in common with existing parts of the company. This might be a florist expanding the business into a garden centre, or a dentist hiring a dental hygienist.
- *Unrelated* diversification adds offerings which have little in common with the rest of the company. An example was BAT Industries, a tobacco company, acquiring Eagle Star, an insurance company. When a company ends up with a number of unrelated activities, it is often called a conglomerate.

Chapter 12 will discuss relatedness in more depth.

Diversification: Young and Mature Businesses

The reader will by now have gathered that this book is cautious and sceptical about the urge to diversify. However, it is important to distinguish between young and growing businesses on the one hand, and mature ones on the other. Great enterprises are created by entrepreneurs with a flair for creating value and serving customers well. They typically start from scratch with a small, backroom or garage business. The business then takes off. The originators find that they can create more and more value by expanding both in volume and in scope. They continue to grow until they reach some optimum size. No book like this would seek to discourage that early stage of expansion. Perhaps we should call this early stage of expansion *enterprise* rather than diversification.

The value generated by diversification after that desirable growth of the young business becomes harder to assess and justify. By the time the business is mature, people who lack the original rare spark of enterprise may direct it. They may be a new generation of family members, or they may be professional managers. They may excel at their jobs, but without the spark of enterprise they may still wish to expand for more questionable reasons. It is at those mature stages that so much over-diversification occurred in parts of the twentieth century, and it is here that we have to be critical and sceptical.

Does the Head Office Add Value?

Corporate strategy is a key responsibility of top management, that is a function of the head office where there is one. However, not all businesses have or need a head office apart from its top line management. A separate head office is only needed by companies complex enough to need several line managers, because the CEO cannot act as sole line manager for the whole company.

Since about 1980 it has become fashionable in companies to ask whether the head office itself 'adds value'. Where a company is complex enough to have a separate head office, that head office will need to discharge certain minimum tasks. They are as follows:

- corporate strategy;
- funding the company in financial markets;
- appointing the management at the next level or levels;
- monitoring performance of divisions and other profit centres; and
- duties imposed by statute or by stock exchanges, such as reporting to investors, complying with company law and other regulations.

In many larger companies the head office performs other functions as well. It might, for example, have central marketing, personnel, purchasing, insurance or research and development functions.

Different companies need different structures, depending on the nature of the business. For example, an engineering contractor's main board needs to approve and then each month review the progress of each major contract that accounts for say 5 per cent or more of the company's annual sales. Again a pharmaceutical giant's head office may contain its research department, which arguably is the company's core value-building activity. However, companies have been known to have central activities that either fail to add value, or positively obstruct value building by the divisions and other profit centres. That is one possible reason for asking whether the head office adds value.

Yet the question can also be raised for an entirely different reason that relates directly to corporate strategy. Does offering O need any head office at all? Or if it does, is this the best head office for it to have? Many a company has been known to add offerings to its collection which would be more valuable outside this company and free from the control of its head office: in other words, if they were either independent or owned by some other company. The addition or retention of such an offering destroys value. More value could be unlocked by its divestment. Superimposing the head office does not add value to such offerings or groups of offerings. It is in this sense that corporate strategy asks whether an offering is one to which the head office adds value.

Chapter 13 will point out one especially powerful reason for questioning the benefit of the head office. The mere existence of the head office must impose some extra costs on any addition to the collection, costs that the new unit would not incur if it remained independent. We call this phenomenon the extra costs of diversified operation. The benefits of adding that extra unit or offering must therefore exceed those extra costs.

Summary

This chapter has set out the essential nature of corporate strategy in an offering-centred strategic framework, and its main issues and tasks. Corporate strategy is essentially the continuous task of monitoring the entire collection of a company's offerings, to see if its value can be improved by additions or divestments. Financial value is the only proper yardstick, not size or growth or risk diversification. We also reject the stakeholder view. We have not yet tackled the issue of relatedness. That is the subject of Chapter 12.

Notes

1. There are many notable examples of the business unit being taken as the unit for corporate strategy. See Porter, M.E. (1985). *Competitive Advantage*. New York: Free Press. Also see Goold, M., Campbell, A. and Alexander, M. (1994). *Corporate-level Strategy*. New York: Wiley. A similar approach is adopted by Collis, D.J. and Montgomery, C.A. (1997). *Corporate Strategy*. Chicago: Irwin.
2. Much of the research evaluated acquisitions. See Bhagat, S., Shleifer, A. and Vishny, R.W. (1990). *Hostile Takeovers in the 1980s: The Return to Corporate Specialization*. Washington: Brookings Papers. Also see Shleifer, A. and Vishny, R.W. (1991). Takeovers in the 60s and the 80s: evidence and implications. *Strategic Management Journal*, **12**(special issue), 51–59. However, the spate of activity during this period was directed at diversifications of any kind, not only acquisitions.
3. For a case history of some of the causes for excessive diversification and the consequences, see Baker, G.P. (1992). Beatrice: a study in the creation and destruction of value. *Journal of Finance*, **XLVII**(3), 1081–1119.
4. Porter, M.E. (1987). From competitive advantage to corporate strategy. *Harvard Business Review*, May–June, pp. 43–59. Also see Sirower, M. (1997). *The Synergy Trap*. New York: Free Press.
5. Waters, R., London, S. and Morrison, S. (2004). Hewlett-Packard wants a foot in every market. Can the company do it all? *Financial Times*, 14 October 2004, p. 17.
6. Sweet revenge of the lady killer, *The Business*, 13/14 February 2005, p. 11.
7. Wright, R. (2004). P&O transforms itself to do what it once did so well – open up world trade. *Financial Times*, 2 November 2004, p. 23.
8. Boles, T. (2005). Takeover on the waterfront. *The Business*, 6/7 November 2005, p. 6.
9. Anslinger, P.L., Klepper, S.J. and Subramaniam, S. (1999). Breaking up. *The McKinsey Quarterly*, **1**, 16–27.
10. Copeland, T., Koller, T. and Murrin, J. (1990). *Valuation: Measuring and Managing the Value of Companies*. New York: Wiley.
11. Burt, T. (2002). Aston Martin chiefs told to change out of bondage gear. *Financial Times*, 26/27 January 2002, p. 26.
12. See Sadtler, D., Campbell, A. and Koch, R. (1998). *Breakup*. Oxford: Capstone.
13. The average basic salary of CEOs of FTSE 100 companies was reported as £800 000 in the year to July 2006. Salaries of chief executives in the

FTSE 250 averaged £500 000 while those of small cap companies was £350 000. See Burgess, K. (2006). Top chief executives see pay rise 30% to £3m. *Financial Times*, 23 November 2006, p. 5.

14. *Financial Times*, 3/4 September 2005, p. 12.
15. Lynn, M. (2005). Why the mega rich rarely get to stay that way for long. *The Business*, 24/25 April 2005, p. 12.
16. For an example of when it finally does, see Baker, G.P. (1992). Beatrice: a study in the creation and destruction of value. *Journal of Finance*, **XLVII**(3), 1081–1119.
17. In vertical integration the addition of an offering may in extreme cases amount to the absorption of one offering by another. For example, a manufacturer of raw 'slab' steel may decide to integrate backwards and acquire its own iron ore mines, but decide against selling any ore to others. On the other hand it may decide to integrate forwards and convert its entire slab production into sheet steel, and thus discontinue the sale of raw steel to external parties.

12

Success in diversification: Relatedness

Introduction

This chapter and the next set out the criteria that corporate strategy should apply to the addition and retention of any offering. Some of these criteria echo those suggested by Michael Porter in 1987,[1] but are here adapted and applied to the offering-centred approach of this book.

The criteria are set out in Figure 12.1.

The better-off test is the fundamental one. It measures whether the offering under review contributes a positive NPV and therefore adds value to the company. Relatedness can be regarded as a condition without which the test cannot be passed. The filters serve to reinforce the better-off test by counteracting specific forms of wishful thinking that have proved consistently disastrous. This book strongly discourages diversifications which do not pass all the criteria, but it equally strongly recommends those that do.

This chapter deals with relatedness, and Chapter 13 with the filters and the test. We suggest that the checks for relatedness and the filters should normally be made before the better-off test is applied. They cost less effort and time than that test. We begin with relatedness, because it is arguably the most important issue in corporate strategy.

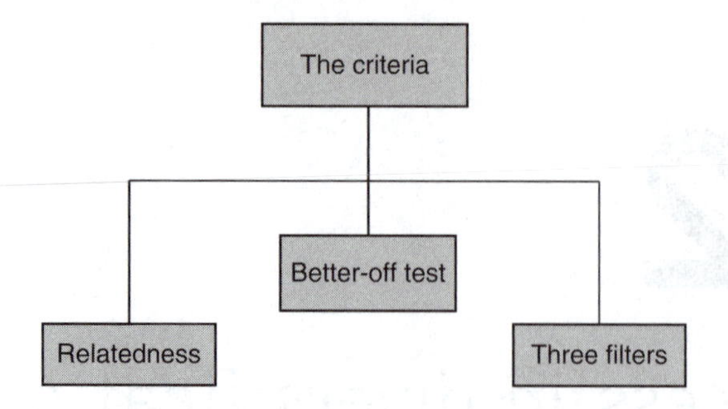

Figure 12.1 The criteria for corporate strategy

Related and Unrelated Diversification

Chapter 11 briefly referred to the diversification spree that characterized large parts of the twentieth century. Much of that diversification was unsuccessful, and most unsuccessful diversifications were unrelated. We call a new offering unrelated if it has no link with the rest of the company. Unrelated diversification tended to be undertaken either for the sake of size as such, or for risk diversification. These unhelpful aims we have examined in Chapter 2, but what matters is that neither of them can in its own right create value.

Diversification creates value only when it exploits links with the rest of the company. There are seven kinds of link, listed and outlined in the next section below. Six of them are links between the new offering and at least one existing offering. The seventh link is between the new offering and the head office. Only when one of these links can build value and is in place is the new offering a related one. Moreover, only a related offering can create value. Relatedness in this sense is an essential condition of passing the better-off test.

The Seven Links of Relatedness

We are so far aware of seven value-building links of relatedness:

1. The *sharing* of significant efforts and resources between various offerings in the collection: much the most common case.

2. Vertical integration: acquiring offering P which uses, or is used by, existing offering O thus substituting an internal for a competitive contractual relationship with a customer or supplier.
3. Complementarity: ensuring the supply of lacking but needed *complementary* offerings.
4. The 'cross-parry': a company launches offering P so as to give indirect protection to its existing offering O.
5. Combining offerings to exploit customer preferences.
6. Combining offerings to improve *market power.*
7. Core collections of certain offerings that need an expert head office as an informed critic.

Figure 12.2 illustrates how links can be either horizontal between two offerings, as in links 1–6, or vertical between an offering and the head office, as in link 7.

Offerings X and Y are horizontally linked with each other. Offering Z has a vertical link with the head office.

As we discuss each type of link, we take P as the offering under review. Should P be added or retained?

Relatedness requires that the link with our existing offering O or with the head office is capable of building significant extra value for the company and that the link should be internal in the sense of ensuring the company's control. If the same value can be achieved say by an external contractual link, then the addition or retention of offering P is not justified. In any case such an offering would fail some of the filters in Chapter 13.

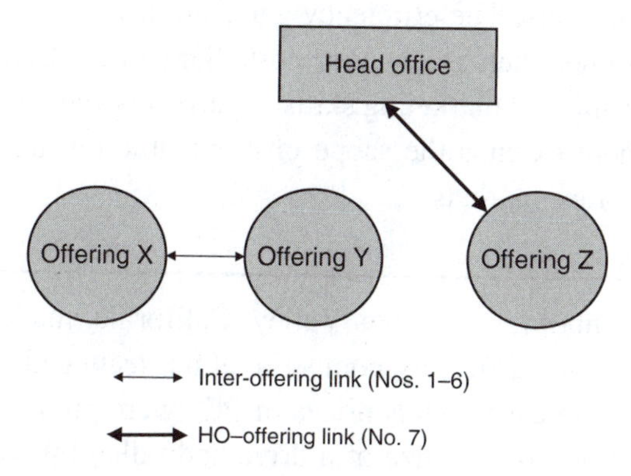

Figure 12.2 Two types of relatedness links

Internalization is not always a matter of formal ownership. For example, where a company is less than 100 per cent or even less than 50 per cent owned, the test is not our shareholding percentage, but whether we are in fact in operational control of achieving the desired benefits of the diversification.

The addition or retention of offering P must of course also pass the other criteria set out in Chapter 13. Relatedness on its own is not enough.

Link 1: Sharing Efforts and Resources

In Link 1, offerings O and P can share efforts and resources and thereby make the company's collection more valuable. This is widely called 'synergy', but we need to describe this sharing more closely. It can occur anywhere in the value chain from inbound logistics to after-sales service.

Link 1 can build value in broadly three ways:

1. A significant saving in unit costs, through economies of scale or perhaps through the exploitation of by-products, such as glycerine from the manufacture of soap. One form of scale economies is the exploitation of unused capacity. Farmers who provide holiday accommodation illustrate this.
2. A significant saving of absolute costs, for example if P brings with it a winning resource which improves the production technology for O. The case of Seagate Technology in the box below is an example.
3. A significant improvement in the quality and attractiveness of O or P to customers. The efficiency gains are used to improve attractiveness, rather than production cost. Sara Lee's transfer of food manufacturing and marketing skills to garments was a case in point.[2] The link here extends the scope of a valuable resource to a wider set of customer markets.

Seagate Technology of Scotts Valley, California, made hard-disk drives, a fiercely competitive, but technically exacting offering. In the early 1990s prices of PCs were plunging. In little over a decade the size of a drive had fallen by two-thirds, its data storage had grown 1,000-fold. In the July–September quarter of 1993 Seagate reported a small, and declining, net profit of $36m on $774m sales. However, it alone among its competitors was not reporting a loss. In 1989 Seagate had decided to become a technological leader. It made a well-targeted acquisition of Imprimis Technology. In 1991 it decided that mastery of a core set of skills was not enough: it must also learn to apply them to more and more offerings. It became a supplier of products for handling text, graphics, audio and video; to supply everything from mass-storage devices to the software for managing databases and networks.

This is a classic example of exploiting a winning resource over enough offerings to achieve needed economies of scale.

(Source: *The Economist*, 13 November 1993)

Link 1 justifies the addition or retention of P only if the potential gain to the company as a whole is

- significant and
- obtainable only if P is part of this company, and the link internalized.

If the resource shared by O and P were merely the canteen, this would not meet the requirement. The saving would not be significant, nor is the need for internalizing the link clear. Nor would our CEO's time qualify as a resource to be shared, unless our CEO happened to have rare skills uniquely needed by P. If P could easily obtain the resource or a substitute capable of producing the same attractions to customers, and do this without passing into our ownership, a proposal to add P would in any case fail some of the filters in Chapter 13.

Link 2: Vertical Integration

The second link, vertical integration, is the merging under single ownership or control of an offering's customer or supplier, with the object of internalizing what would otherwise be an arm's length contractual relationship. An example is a dentist hiring her own dental mechanic.

Vertical integration had a great vogue in parts of the twentieth century. Automobile assemblers integrated backward into making their own components, and crude oil producers integrated forward into refining and petrol retailing.

A large number of vertical integrations have failed. The 'market-instead' filter of Chapter 13 is a stiff test designed precisely to question vertical integration proposals. However, vertical integration is not invariably wrong. It can build value in three sets of circumstances:

a. In a thin market, by securing the continuity of a needed relationship which might otherwise be precarious.
b. Again in a thin market, by denying the link to competitors: News Corporation bought 20th Century Fox in order to get control of its library of vintage films from the golden age of the cinema.
c. By ensuring quality where one of the two parties' tight specification or difficult process requires the extra degree of control conferred by the one-to-one relationship of an internal link: an example might be a market garden owned by a specialist restaurant or gourmet food shop. As in the other cases, this is a valid case for vertical integration, as long as internalization is essential to its success.

The main drawback of vertical integration is that the internalized relationship loses its competitive spur. Its pitfalls will be more fully discussed in Chapter 13 when we discuss the 'market-instead' filter.

Link 3: Complementarity

Complementary offering P is for our purposes linked to existing offering O if

a. O would be useless to customers unless they can also purchase P; and
b. P has no significant substitutes, for example, because it has a specification customized for O.

The link is only a short step away from O and P being components of a single offering.

Nalebuff and Bradenburger in their book *Co-opetition* give an example that seems to meet these conditions.[3] In 1986, Nintendo launched its new video game system called the Nintendo Entertainment System in the United States. A security chip built into the cut-price hardware ensured that Nintendo controlled the cartridges that could be run on the system. Initially, Nintendo provided customers with a carefully chosen selection of game cartridges designed by its own ace designer. The games constituted a complementary offering which Nintendo had to provide to get the system working.

Nintendo did not long remain the only provider of games though it exercised great control, by contractual and other means, over market developments. Once sales had taken off other software houses were licensed to write games that could run on Nintendo's hardware. Licensees were prohibited from releasing the same title for other video game systems for 2 years. Nintendo also retained control over the number and the quality of the games developed by licensees and also manufactured the cartridges. Though Nintendo's practices later came under scrutiny from an antitrust perspective the sales of both the hardware and the games boomed.

Where substitutes are freely available, just being complements no longer constitutes a link that can build value or which needs to be internalized. A manufacturer of motorcars has normally no need to ensure that petrol is available. A manufacturer of printers need not usually worry about ensuring the supply of paper.

If both conditions (a) and (b) are met, a link is established, but as the Nintendo case suggests, whether internalization of the link is justified, depends on whether internalization is the best option.

Link 4: The Cross-Parry

The cross-parry is a rare phenomenon.

A company launches offering P not as a value-builder in its own right, but in order to protect the value of its existing offering O, which is under attack. The new offering P need not build value in its own right, but its investment must clearly show a positive NPV for O, the threatened offering, and P combined.

The classic case is that of Goodyear, as told by Hamel & Prahalad.[4] Tyres are not a global offering. They are costly to transport, and best made relatively close to the customer. The list of sellers tends to vary from country to country. Global market leaders often encounter local competitors. Michelin's most profitable offering around 1970 was automobile tyres in the European market. Goodyear's was its tyres – offering O – in the US home market. However, in the early 1970s, Michelin attacked that US market. Goodyear decided that its best countermove was to launch tyres – protective offering P – in Europe so as to threaten or attack Michelin's prime source of cash flow. In the event, Goodyear failed to stop Michelin's attack on the US market, but at least it slowed it down.

A more recent case is that of Dell and Hewlett-Packard (HP).[5] HP's profits at the time were for the most part made by its printers. HP was also, however, seriously competing in the PC market after acquiring Compaq in 2002. At that time, Dell was the only clearly profitable PC manufacturer. The *Financial Times* of 14 October 2004 reported that Dell had 'taken aim at HP's core source of profits by launching its own line of printers'.

The conditions in which the cross-parry is likely to occur are rare. They appear to apply mainly where two intense rivals are each capable of playing a significant spoiling role in more than one of each other's circular or oligopolistic markets.

Link 5: Exploiting Customer Preferences

In some cases customers prefer to buy two offerings from the same seller. An example is the retailer of security equipment. Customers prefer the retailer also to provide installation and servicing. Likewise users of Gillette's Sensor razors may prefer to buy replacement blades made by Gillette rather than a much smaller rival.[6]

In other cases offering O is more attractive through the existence and easy accessibility, or simply the proximity of another offering P. Thus a novel may sell better if it is the subject of a successful Hollywood film. A management book on strategy may be more attractive if the author also conducts executive workshops. Again, a supermarket and a petrol filling station may each attract more customers if they are located together on the same site.

By themselves these advantages do not constitute relatedness. They can do that only where they can build value and the link needs to be internalized under the same ownership. That is by no means always the case.

Link 6: Joining Offerings to Improve Market Power

Chapter 7 discussed the fairly common case where a few players, due to some barriers to entry, dominate a market. We called such markets circular or oligopolistic. Each seller in the dominant group will have a significant share of the whole market. Link 6 applies where one seller can improve its market power and margins by acquiring one of the others.

Examples are a local newsagent buying its nearest rival, one of the oil majors acquiring one of the others, or a commuter rail company buying a local bus company. There are often regulatory barriers to such monopoly-seeking actions. Again, it is by no means certain that the acquisition would result in improved margins: for example, customers may react adversely. However, where the acquisition is feasible and capable of building value, the diversification is a related one.

The link can be indirect. A supermarket might buy a redundant nearby branch of a bank and redevelop it as a fitness club in order to prevent it being acquired by a rival supermarket. Again the motive is to boost market share compared with what that share would be after the arrival of a nearby competitor. Such an acquisition might, however, fail the best-owner filter in Chapter 13.

A circular market like these can of course be a private market (Chapter 6) if the offerings are differentiated. In that case each offering will have a market with different boundaries from its substitutes, but in each such market there is nonetheless a measurable market share.

Finally, link 6 can apply where there are few buyers, instead of few sellers. The technical jargon for this is monopsony or oligopsony, instead of monopoly or oligopoly. The owner of 50 per cent of all cinemas in an area could increase its bargaining power with film distributors if it were able to step up its share to 90 per cent without triggering regulatory countermeasures. Similarly, a high concentration in the grocery business could put undue pressure on the suppliers of milk and dairy products.

Link 7: Joining Offerings Under an Expert Head Office

Some offerings need an expert head office. In links 1–6 the links are *between* offerings. The head office is not needed in its own right.

It is simply a roof for offerings that need to be in the same house for other reasons. When none of the seven links are present, so that the offerings are unrelated, then there is no inherent reason why each offering should not be an independent company quoted on a stock exchange. Assuming that each offering is large enough to be listed on a stock market as an independent company, that market could quite adequately put a value on the company that owns it and on any future capital that it may wish to raise. It could also act as a financial authority to discipline the company, should it fail to perform. The market and its institutions perform these functions for listed companies. Stock markets are able to assess a company's performance and prospects, because the information they receive from that company is transparent and prompt enough for that purpose.

Smaller offerings would not be listed on a stock exchange, but the lack of a liquid capital market may well be balanced by the freedom from bureaucracy enjoyed by small, independent businesses. Unless it has a high degree of monopoly, its competitive market will discipline poor performance, with its bank and other creditors assessing its credit rating and thus replacing the stock market.

Link 7 is for offerings whose value and prospects are much more opaque than the average. That is because they are

- *either* investment-intensive as in nuclear power generation;
- *or* technically complex, as in biotechnology;
- *or* long-fuze: with a very long gestation and payback period, as in ethical drugs.

The stock market would of course eventually become aware of any shortcomings in such a company's performance, but the symptoms would only become apparent after a damaging period of delay, and after an unacceptably large loss of value. For that reason the securities of such a company would attract an unnecessarily high risk factor. The cost of capital would be high. That delay can instead be materially reduced by a head office which the market accepts as sufficiently expert in that company's special risks.

That expert head office therefore needs to be closer to the action than the stock market, better and more promptly informed and better qualified in the specific nature and risks of the offering. It also of course needs to be privy to the framing and execution of any strategy.

The researchers who drew attention to this requirement are Gould and Campbell.[7]

The collection of offerings assembled by such a company needs to be a 'core' collection, in the sense that all the offerings should be within the specialized expertise of the head office.

Link 7 is thus the unusual case in which the link arises from the role of the head office, not from some affinity between offerings. Without the head office these offerings would be less valuable.

This completes our account of the seven links of relatedness that we have found.

Relatedness is Not a Matter of 'Industry' Membership

In equating relatedness with the presence of one of the seven links, we reject the predominant traditional view of relatedness. This treats business activities as related if they belong to some common category, such as 'an industry' or to a particular class in an industrial classification scheme, such as the Standard Industrial Classification (SIC). This predominant approach is popular with researchers because industrial classifications are so widely known, and so easy to apply.[8] Managers are generally not tempted to go down that road, because they can see that the commonalities in the SIC categories are too abstract and rigid to do justice to the facts. Relatedness should be seen in bottom-up, not top-down, terms. Two offerings may, for example, be related, if they attract the same customers or use the same kind of resources without being in the same industry.

Cinemas found early in their development that they could very profitably sell ice cream and other refreshments. Entertainment and catering are not in the same industry. Similarly, Saga in the United Kingdom marketed holidays to pensioners but then moved into motor and household insurance for the same clientele.[9] Saga had become expert in pensioners' approaches to buying decisions and also to their risk profiles. This gave Saga an advantage in the two classes of insurance.

The Sunday Times on 28 November 2004 reported that Tesco, the British supermarket giant, had turned its sights to the media industry.[10] It was selling advertising space in its supermarkets, car parks, lorries and so on, and had sent out hundreds of brochures to potential advertisers, among them its own suppliers.

Ocado, which successfully started up in 2003 as an online retailer of groceries in parts of the United Kingdom, effectively offered superior retail software combined with a thorough understanding of what its targeted customers wished to buy, and how. Ocado's is a typical turn-of-the-century offering, in which information management plays as big a role as the actual nature of what is sold. If Ocado had decided to acquire a specialized software house of its own, that would have counted as related, although software would surely not have been within its industry classification. Whether it would have passed all our other criteria in Chapter 13 is another matter: the software offering might well have failed, for example the 'market-instead' filter in that chapter. It would not, however, have passed the SIC test of relatedness. The SIC and similar classifications are generally declining in their usefulness. Offerings are less and less classifiable by 'industries' in the traditional sense.

Another example of relatedness across conventional industry boundaries is Seagate Technology, in a box earlier in this chapter.

This SIC-type view of relatedness is both too wide and too narrow. Oil drilling and petrol stations are both in the petroleum industry, but it does not follow that they would benefit from being owned or marketed by the same company. On the other hand, a petrol station and a supermarket may well benefit from being owned on the same site by the same company if this helped either or both to attract more customers.

Other Defective Concepts of Relatedness

Nevertheless, once the industry test of relatedness is dropped, there are other risks of drawing the boundaries of relatedness too widely. Banks and pubs both use retail outlets, but that would not make a merger between a bank and a chain of pubs related. We ourselves have above suggested that a head office with special skills can be a link of relatedness (Link 7 in our list), but only for special categories of offerings that need a special kind of head office. That is in our view not a very common case.

At the same time the mere fact that a head office has a highly developed skill for 'parenting' or supervising wide categories of offerings is not in our view enough to justify us in treating any such offering as being related.[11] The test is whether the offering needs the head office, and that test is in our view passed only in the conditions of Link 7. If parenting skills were enough to establish relatedness, conglomerates would pass as related collections of offerings. The term 'related' would become indistinguishable from 'unrelated', and lose its thrust. The purpose of introducing the relatedness test is to restrict diversification to offerings, which exploit the company's very own skills and opportunities. That is why we define relatedness as meaning the presence of at least one of a small number of links which have in practice been found to be potential value-builders.

How Far Does any Head Office Need to Understand Its Offerings?

Link 7 describes a special set of offerings which need a head office that understands their risks and opportunities quite intimately, intimately enough to share in the framing of strategy. That case should be distinguished from the generality of simpler offerings, which do not require that degree of detailed understanding or strategy framing by the head office.

However, no offering is so simple that the head office needs no understanding whatever of how it ticks and what its risks are. Risk is at the heart of this issue. All commercial enterprise has risks, for example competitive risks and credit risks, and a head office as the internal funding authority needs at least to know what worst case risk an offering might constitute to the company as a whole. Hoover's British subsidiary in 1992 came close to ruining its US parent with a promotion which offered customers free flights. It is possible that the US parent was too remote to be aware of the state of competition in the UK market for domestic appliances, but maybe the parent would have done better to be less remote.

Head offices therefore all of them need a minimum grasp of their offerings, but this minimum requirement applies to all head offices. Without it the head office becomes an impediment; a bad owner and a destroyer of value. However, it does not create relatedness with any offering. Link 7 concerns a special type of offering, for which the head office needs to perform an essential service by virtue of its much deeper understanding of that offering, far beyond a mere minimum grasp of its risks.

The Company's Scope

Many companies define their 'scope'. They ask, what business are we in? An answer might be 'in designing, manufacturing and marketing drugs for medical applications' or 'in retailing food and household goods'. The benefit of such a definition is negative rather than positive. It seeks to ban activities or skills, the risks of which the head office is not competent to supervise or in which the company is unlikely to excel. Such a definition is of course strategic in nature, but it is not itself a strategy. It is not by itself a guide to adding value. It is a useful guide to intermediate unit managers of the fields in which the company does not propose to add offerings, for one of the two reasons just stated.

The tendency of companies to define their scope may well be a response to the drawbacks of complexity. 'Complexity' in this book denotes a structure in which top managers are not close to all the company's manifold customers and customer markets. Complexity comes from the drive for size. Statements defining scope seek to control the diversity of technologies and customer markets, in this case with an eye on avoiding too many disparate risks.

To the extent that the scope issue is seen as restricting the variety of risks, it has little in common with the concept of relatedness. Offerings outside the company's scope may easily fall within one of the links of relatedness other than Link 7, and by no means all offerings within the company's scope will have such links. The company may nevertheless wish to use its scope as a further constraint on its diversification, but that leaves intact the need to avoid unrelated offerings.

Summary

Relatedness is a matter of bottom-up links, not top-down SIC or similar classifications. Seven types of links have been specified.

We suggest that an offering should not be added or retained unless it is linked to another offering by one of Links 1–6, or to the head office by Link 7. On the other hand, relatedness is just a necessary condition, not a sufficient one. It is one condition of passing the better-off test described in Chapter 13. For the offering to be added, it also needs to pass that test and all three filters also described in that chapter. For it to be retained, it needs to pass the test and two of those filters.

Notes

1. Porter, M.E. (1987). From competitive advantage to corporate strategy. *Harvard Business Review*, May–June, pp. 43–59.
2. *The Economist*, 14 November 1992.
3. Nalebuff, B.J. and Brandenburger, A.M. (1996). *Co-opetition*. London: HarperCollinsBusiness.
4. Hamel, G. and Prahalad, C.K. (1985). Do you really have a global strategy? *Harvard Business Review*, July–August, pp. 139–148.
5. Waters, R., London, S. and Morrison, S. (2004). Hewlett-Packard wants a foot in every market. Can the company do it all? *Financial Times*, 14 October 2004, p. 17.
6. Such competition for replacement parts raises some interesting legal issues, see Tait, N. (2005). Razor ruling cuts into trademark armour. *Financial Times*, 24 March 2005, p. 13.
7. Goold, M. and Campbell, A. (1987). *Strategies and Styles*. Oxford: Blackwell. Their term for this kind of involvement by the head office is 'strategic planning'.
8. Robins, J. and Wiersema, M.F. (1995). A resource-based approach to the multibusiness firm. *Strategic Management Journal*, **16**, 277–299.
9. John, P. (2004). Saga to cash in on blurring of perception and reality. *Financial Times*, 14/15 August 2004, p. M4.
10. Fletcher, R. (2004). Tesco TV takes on the media. *The Sunday Times*, 28 November 2004, Business section, p. 9.
11. Such cases have been made. See, for example, Prahalad, C.K. and Bettis, R.A. (1986). The dominant logic: a new linkage between diversity and performance. *Strategic Management Journal*, **7**, 485–501.

13

Success in diversification: The filters and the better-off test

Introduction: The Diversification Binge of the 1960s and 1970s

A recurring theme of our review of corporate strategy is that companies should not aim at size or complexity. They should enhance and build on their own inherent excellence, and avoid the me-tooism of trying to imitate the excellence of their competitors. Companies should be simple and transparent in their scope. Fritz Schumacher coined the phrase 'small is beautiful'.[1] As already suggested in Chapter 1, we add 'simple is beautiful'. Readers are reminded that the reason for this ascetic sounding advice is that the very popular opposite view has again and again ended in disaster – it does not work!

The sceptical reader may be tempted to point to examples of current or even past conglomerates which appear successful. Caution is needed with such examples:

- The drawbacks of complexity often take time to appear.
- Corporate raiders like Hanson in the 1970s and 1980s often had long periods of value creation. This was a reward not for complexity, but for buying assets cheap and selling them dear. Hence the running of the unrelated retained businesses was neither these raiders' primary activity nor the main source of their successes.

- In other cases the results of one part of the business are so outstanding that they hide cans of worms in others. In these cases divestments would have made the success even greater.
- Finally, there are some managers who are so brilliant that they can make a success even of a conglomerate. General Electric has been an example of this for many years. That is an exception that proves the rule. Mere mortals are best advised to abide by the rules: rule-breaking is for superfolk. It takes exceptional brilliance to overcome the drawbacks of inappropriate complexity. Success in such special cases comes not from the creation of a conglomerate, but from the exceptional talents of the management.

We have so far noted that the retention or addition of an offering is justified only if the offering is a related one, as set out in Chapter 12, and if it has a positive NPV. That last point is the essence of the better-off test mentioned in Chapters 11 and 12. This chapter digs deeper into the nature of that test and reinforces it with three filters designed to counteract the widespread tendency to over-diversify.

The need for stiffening the requirements was strongly argued by Michael Porter in 1987.[2] That date is not a coincidence. It came at the end of some two decades of a diversification spree in which companies had pursued the false goal of size with devastating consequences. Most of the diversification was unrelated. The vast majority was unsuccessful. Many acquisitions had to be redivested.

The Costs of Diversified Operation

Chapter 11 briefly referred to the extra costs of diversified operation. The mere existence of the head office as a separate entity imposes additional costs. Its mere existence makes for longer lines of communication, imposes bureaucratic uniformity, dilutes the sense of responsibility of unit line managers and demotivates them and their employees. If an offering or other unit were independent, all decisions would need to be taken within it. Once the unit ceases to be independent, some responsibilities pass to the head office, thus diluting the spirit of enterprise and local accountability for results. This is an inherent consequence of diversified operation. The resulting inefficiencies and missed opportunities are a cost not borne by simpler competitors.

These added costs are not captured by the reporting system, and are to that extent concealed and hard to quantify. Hence they are widely ignored. These costs are, however, likely to be substantial, even in the best-structured companies. Worse, when new activities do not have the benefit of relatedness (examined in Chapter 12), they are even less likely to be balanced by benefits. The company's financial value will suffer. Its vulnerability to hostile takeover or insolvency will rise. This is not what suits either managers or investors. Both have a strong interest in avoiding these extra costs unless they are outweighed by benefits.

The extra costs of diversified operation are a serious factor in corporate strategy, and a recurring theme in this chapter. Once again we see why small, and above all simple is beautiful!

The Test and the Filters

In this book we look at corporate strategy in terms of offerings. That makes corporate strategy a matter of adding, retaining or divesting offerings. For a valid decision to add or retain an offering, that offering needs to pass the better-off test, which adapts a test of that name recommended by Michael Porter.[3] In any case offerings need to be related ones, as discussed in Chapter 12. Relatedness, it will be recalled, is an important condition of passing the better-off test.

However, the better-off test can be and regularly is performed with rose-tinted spectacles. If those conducting the analysis have the prevailing bias in favour of getting bigger, they tend to prepare an optimistic set of future cash flows, or to use an inadequate discount factor. To correct for that optimistic bias in decisions to *add* offerings, we further apply three filters:

- the market-instead filter;
- the best-owner filter; and
- the robustness filter.

A decision to *retain* rather than add an offering would have to meet only two of the filters. It would not need to pass the robustness filter, because retain-or-divest decisions occur later in the life of an offering. If the offering then fails the better-off test or either of the other two filters, it should be divested.

We shall now describe and discuss these criteria, summarized in Figure 12.1.

The Better-Off Test

Chapter 12 stressed that the better-off test cannot be passed if the offering is not a related one. Apart from that the test simply requires that the company as a whole must be financially more valuable with the offering than without it.

The stress on the whole company is important. The test can seldom be applied to just one offering as a free-standing entity. The proposed new offering is very likely to affect the unit costs of other offerings. It may also have a positive or negative effect on the sales of other offerings, possibly in remote parts of the company. Sometimes two or more offerings are so interdependent that add or retain decisions can only be taken about them collectively even though their competitive positions are distinct and must be separately analysed.

The practical details in applying the test are as follows:

- The comparison is between the NPV of the entire company (a) with and (b) without offering O. The 'without' scenario should of course take account of likely future changes in the environment, such as O's acquisition by a competitor if we do not acquire it. The 'without' scenario must also be the best alternative available to the company. This might, for example, be simply to discontinue the offering, or to sell it to a competitor, or to replace it with an updated and improved version. If the decision is between retention and divestment, the price at which it is sold must be assumed to be the best price obtainable in the market.
- Values and discount factors applied should be those which the stock market would apply if it had the same inside information as the company has.
- A new or retained offering may give the company realistic *options* to add further valuable offerings at future dates. Divestment would entail the loss of those options. Operating options of this kind have an option value in the technical sense, as do market-traded currency or other financial options. Such option values should be included

in the analysis, but conservatively. They tend to be significant, for example, in the petroleum industry.

- The transaction costs of acquiring or divesting must be accounted for, as well as the purchase or sale price.
- An acquisition of another company or any part of it normally acquires more than the targeted offering O. The smallest unit available for purchase may, for example, be a division of another company. The cost of O in the analysis must allow for the total cost of what is acquired, less what can be realized from disposals (net after the costs of disposal), less the positive or plus the negative value to the company of what may be neither wanted nor disposable.
- The extra costs of diversified operation are very hard to quantify, but that is no excuse for ignoring them. An estimate must be made and included. These costs are added by an acquisition, and should be saved by a divestment. The estimated costs or savings should be assessed with a measure of pessimism. This is essential as an antidote to the endemic bias towards size.

Optimism is a serious risk in all diversification proposals. Such proposals often generate a sense of elation and euphoria in which normal caution and circumspection are forgotten. The strategist must constantly remember that most corporate disasters of recent years are due to damaging acquisitions and other diversifications.

However, in essence the better-off test is a simple, easily grasped concept. No offering should be added or retained unless the company will be more valuable with it than without it.

Why the Filters?

The three filters serve to reinforce the caution needed in applying the better-off test. They correct the widespread bias towards optimism, and towards ignoring or downplaying the extra costs of diversified operation. The introduction of these filters is therefore a pragmatic corrective to a deep-seated tendency to over-diversify. If this tendency had not been so pervasive, the better-off test on its own should have been enough. A level-headed analyst would apply the cautious spirit of these filters as part of the better-off test.

The *market-instead filter* discourages unnecessary vertical integration. Vertical integration is the internalizing of what would otherwise be an arm's length market transaction between buyer and supplier. We encountered it in Link 2 in Chapter 12.

The *best-owner filter* invalidates the acquisition or retention of an offering which would be more valuable either independent or under the ownership of another business.

The *robustness filter* serves to ensure that a proposed new offering retains strong prospects of durable value creation. It guards against optimism about the length of time that an offering can continue to build value despite various threats. Enterprise is not possible without risk-taking, but risks need to be carefully selected and controlled.

The Market-Instead Filter

The market-instead filter requires a critical review of vertical integration proposals, which are also the subject of Link 2 in Chapter 12. The filter requires that a supplier–customer relationship should only be brought in-house, that is be internalized, if a normal market relationship is for some reason either not available at all or at any rate not sufficiently competitive. A manufacturer of small motors for vacuum cleaners and other appliances should normally have neither its own foundry nor its own vacuum cleaner plant. Its own foundry would be backward integration into a supplier. Its own vacuum cleaner manufacturer would be forward integration into a customer.

Vertical integration has many drawbacks. One of the two offerings obtains a captive, in-house customer. That tends to lose other potential customers, who will – correctly or incorrectly – suspect that their internally owned or controlled competitor buys on preferential terms. Worse still, vertical integration removes or reduces the internal supplier's spur to be competitive. Captive customers are seldom served as keenly as arm's length ones. Similarly, the internal buyer may not have the right or the urge to shop around for the best-value supplier. Head offices are by no means always enlightened enough to leave their units free to buy from external sources. This lack of a competitive spur is a simple consequence of *internalizing* what might otherwise be a competitive market relationship. Internalization is what causes the damage.

This filter can, however, be passed if the alternative of a competitive arm's length relationship is not available. The concept of 'market failure' may be helpful here. If there is no adequate competitive market, then internalization is often the least bad alternative. Market failure may be absolute. A surgeon pioneering a new technique in brain surgery may need a theatre nurse trained by herself; she could not safely use an agency nurse instead. The needed skills are simply not generally available. Sometimes market failure is a matter of degree. The surgical technique may not be unique, but still require a very high level of nursing skill. An agency nurse would not be wholly inappropriate, but the hospital might still be training nurses to a higher standard of skill, and have good quality control reasons to insist on employing its own specially trained staff to avoid failures. In other words the market exists, but not at an adequate level of quality.

This case for internalization can of course succeed only

- where there is an absolute scarcity of a type of resource such as 20th Century Fox's film library so that an acquisition at an economic price acquires a scarce resource and denies it to others; or
- where the nature of the offering requires exceptionally high or tailor-made quality of performance, as is illustrated in the nursing example; or
- where forward integration is needed to overcome resistance by powerful prospective customers to an innovative offering, as is illustrated by Alcoa's and Reynolds' decision in the 1960s to make cans themselves in order to establish their new aluminium-using process.[4]

The filter serves to prevent internalization where it is not the best available solution.

The Best-Owner Filter

The best-owner filter requires the company to be the best owner of a new or retained offering O. The 'best' owner is the one that can generate the most value from the offering. In other words, if the offering has a greater NPV in the hands of another owner, or independent, then we must not add it to our collection, nor retain it.

This filter too is a reinforcement and extension of the better-off test. A new offering may indeed slip through the better-off test, yet fail this filter. If the offering is a new one, then have we really made realistic assumptions about the actions of competitors, such as a better owner in the sense just described? We come back to horse sense, defined as the quality that stops horses betting on human beings. As we are all human, our NPV projections may well have erred on the side of optimism. The filter forces on us the discipline of estimating the NPV of the offering to alternative owners. The process may lead us to discover some shaky assumptions in our own calculations.

If, on the other hand, the offering is an existing one, its retention would not be the best option open to the company. More value would be generated by its sale for more than its NPV to us. The case of Worthwhile Hotels in Chapter 11 illustrated this.

In Chapter 12, we noted the need for the head office to have a minimum understanding of the economics and the risks of each offering. If by any chance our head office lacks that minimum understanding about offering O, then we cannot be the best owner.

This filter can in some cases save the company from vulnerability to takeover. If O accounts for an appreciable proportion of the value of our entire company, and is seriously more valuable to, say, competitor C, then it pays C to bid for our company, and then divest all our other assets except O. C will have acquired O very cheaply! In 1986, Quaker Oats acquired Anderson Clayton because Quaker wanted to acquire its Gaines dog food business. It sold off all the other businesses of Anderson, retaining just Gaines. A clear gain?

The Robustness Filter

The better-off test requires the offering to generate value for the payback period as a whole. The robustness filter goes further and requires that a new offering generates value for the greater of (a) the payback period and (b) the lead time needed to abort or divest the offering in the event of shock news. Shocks can come from competitors, from customers themselves moving away from the preferences served by the offering, or from non-market events like social discord or political change. Any of these can impair robustness. Moreover, the company may be slow to abort or divest in response to any of these shocks. The tendency is for managers to be too committed either internally or in the eyes of the outside world to contemplate a U-turn.

The offering needs to be tested for robustness against shocks that come both before and after the cost of capital has been recovered. If competitive conditions make divestment imperative at a very early stage in the life of an offering, a delay may result in a severe loss of value. The case need not be much better if the need to divest becomes apparent soon after the recovery of the cost of capital. If the investment was £10 million, and the company recovers this and another £5 million, but then loses £30 million, the offering will not have improved the company's value.

This filter is not required for a decision to retain – rather than add – offering O. That retain-or-divest decision tends to occur significantly later in the life of the offering, when it already has a track record and U-turns are no longer an issue.

One of the purposes of the filter is to ensure that the protective armour, which two of the cornerstones (matchless and inseparable) of a winning resource bring to the new offering, is robust enough to protect against loss of value even in unexpectedly adverse circumstances. Like the other filters, it counters the tendency to apply the better-off test too optimistically.

Summary

This chapter has presented the better-off test and its three filters which must be passed by any proposal for a new offering to be added to the collection. The same criteria apply to the retention of an existing offering, with the exception of the robustness filter. Between them, the criteria are a strong discipline designed to help in the pursuit of value-seeking diversification and to counteract the observed tendency to destroy value by over-diversification or reluctance to divest.

A Look Back at Corporate Strategy

Corporate strategy continuously monitors the company's collection of offerings, making decisions to add, retain or divest offerings with a view to improving the value of the collection as a whole. Like competitive strategy, corporate strategy must be single-minded in pursuing the objective of financial value. In addition, it must avoid the aim of size for its own sake, and avoid unnecessary complexity.

The company's collection of offerings maximizes value if it pursues only

- profitable customers; and
- offerings at which the company excels.

There is a history of unsuccessful diversification, suggesting that top managements are not selective enough in adding offerings, and too slow and reluctant to divest them. Timely divestment can add or preserve substantial value.

The addition of any offering can therefore be justified only if they pass the better-off test and the three filters. The better-off test can only be passed if the proposed new offering is related to the rest of the company through one of the links of relatedness. Relatedness is not a matter of belonging to the same SIC class or similar classification.

The retention of any offering also has to pass the better-off test, including the relatedness condition, but only two of the three filters.

Decisions often have to be taken about more than one offering, where these are interdependent.

That ends Part 4 and our review of corporate strategy. Chapter 15 will discuss nuts and bolts: the implications for structuring and managing companies for this task.

Notes

1. Schumacher, E.F. (1993). *Small is Beautiful*. London: Vintage Books.
2. Porter, M.E. (1987). From competitive advantage to corporate strategy. *Harvard Business Review*, May–June, pp. 43–59.
3. Ibid.
4. Bower, J.L., Bartlett, C.A., Christensen, C.R., Pearson, A.E. and Andrews, K.R. (1991). Crown cork and seal case. *Business Policy: Text and Cases*. Seventh edition. Homewood, Illinois: Irwin. pp. 126–147.

PART 5

Organizing and Structuring for Offering-Centred Strategies

This book has proposed strategies for *offerings*. This new approach to strategy causes little difficulty and few tensions in small and simple businesses. However, in more complex businesses it affects how such businesses need to be organized and structured.

Part 5 deals with the practical implications of this framework for how businesses are run and structured. Chapter 14 does this for competitive strategy, and Chapter 15 for corporate strategy.

14

Offerings need sponsors

The Problem: Offerings as the Unit

Our framework for business strategy is centred on *offerings*. The case for the offering as the strategic unit is presented in Chapter 1. Briefly, what makes or breaks a competitive business is customer choice. What customers choose is the offering, not some management unit like a division or a profit centre. Hence the vital strategic trick is to design and market offerings which customers will choose at price/volume levels that build value for our company.

It goes without saying that costs need to be competitive if offerings are to build value. However, even the most brilliant cost controls will fail to create value unless customers are sufficiently attracted by what we offer to sell them. Our cost-effectiveness is within our own control, but our customers and competitors are not.

Organization units have to be designed for predominantly internal tasks: the management of assets, resources and costs. Offerings by contrast need to be shaped with an eye on external parties: customers and competitors. The need to design strategies for offerings, but organize the business for managing assets and costs, tends to cause conflict between managers with diverging responsibilities in complex companies. The offering can get lost in that conflict. This chapter proposes a practical resolution of that conflict in the shape of an internal *sponsor* for each offering.

That conflict may not plague small or simple businesses with few or closely related offerings. For example, a sole owner/manager may well be in charge of all the offerings and also of the assets, resources and costs. Simple businesses with few offerings will also not need sponsors, as we suggest in this chapter. Even for them, however, it is vital to attend to the competitive positioning of each offering, and not all managers do that naturally. Hence the principles and suggestions set out in this chapter should be instructive even where there is no conflict between managers with diverging responsibilities.

The Tasks of Competitive Strategy

Competitive strategy covers four management tasks:

1. design of a new offering;
2. approval of the project to produce, resource and fund the offering;
3. implementation; and
4. monitoring.

The structural conflict between inward- and outward-facing responsibilities is likely to cause the most trouble where there is a number of managers with conflicting responsibilities.

Even in a large company it takes relatively few managers to discharge tasks 1, 2 and 4. The *design* of a new offering is for a few relatively senior people who are close to markets and to the customers and competitors in those markets. Its *approval* is the task of top management, and therefore of even fewer people.

Monitoring the progress of an offering is again a task for relatively few people. Monitoring is a task that begins at the same time as implementation. Even before an offering is in place to be sold to customers, its progress to that stage needs to be monitored against intended progress milestones, cost assumptions and features designed to attract profitable customers. As offerings may need resources from outside their own management units, the monitoring task too can therefore involve conflict, but is not itself the cause of conflict.

Implementation is the Crux

Tasks 1, 2 and 4 therefore do not necessarily cause conflict between strategy tasks and organization structure, because they need not cut across normal lines of responsibility. However, implementation –

Task 3 – can cause conflict. Implementation, unlike the other three stages, can involve numerous managers in many of the functions of the business. Moreover, implementation of the original design is crucial to the success of every offering. No new offering is likely to generate value unless it is delivered in such a way as to attract the intended customers at the intended price and time. To entrust its delivery to managers in a different management unit from where it was designed, beyond the influence of those who designed it, is a recipe for failure.

Implementation is for practical purposes part and parcel of day-to-day management. The characteristic tasks and problems of implementation are not primarily strategic. The reason why implementation is the crux of our conflict is that no strategy can build value unless it is delivered with intimate awareness of the competitive intent that underlies each competitive strategy, each planned new offering. Whoever is in charge of delivering a new offering must 'own' its design and concept. That is not a natural priority in day-to-day management. Continuity is needed between design and delivery, and that continuity does not come naturally. Designers have different skills from operating managers. Continuity has to be deliberately put in place. That is what makes implementation the crux of the problem we tackle in this chapter.

The Design Problem: Few Units, Many Offerings

The main conflict is, as we have seen, between an outward-looking design task and an at least partly inward-looking delivery task. There is one other conflict. There are few large companies with only one or two offerings. An example might be a simple company whose single offering at a given time is the design and construction of a single nuclear power station. This is not, however, the prevailing pattern. Many businesses have dozens or hundreds of offerings, yet at the same time their assets, resources and costs are most effectively grouped into a few, perhaps less than a dozen management units.

A central issue here is that each offering needs the continuity of being 'owned' by a single person through all its stages from design to delivery and beyond. How can such a person be fitted into the management unit structure?

The Solution: A Sponsor for Each Offering

The solution we propose for these conflicts is that each offering should have a *sponsor* with continuity of commitment from design to delivery and beyond. The job of sponsor will sound unfamiliar and odd, and raise many questions. So let us describe it by posing some of these questions.

What exactly are the tasks of the sponsor for each offering?
The sponsor is in sole charge of the design of each offering and of monitoring its implementation. The sponsor is not, however, in charge, let alone in sole charge of implementation. If they were, they would not be needed! They must constantly draw the attention of those responsible to any slippage of time, to any failure to attain the competitive aims of the design and to any cost overruns that might impair the value to be created by the offering. They will also be in close touch with the intended market and suggest ways of overcoming new threats and exploiting new opportunities in that market. They may well have the unit general manager as their boss, but they have functions which are independent of that person's functions. That is not an easy relationship, but the need for it stems from the inherent tension between internal and external pressures in business.

How many sponsors?
The number of sponsors must depend on how 'big' the offerings are. In the normal case, where the company has a number of offerings, none of them of giant size, there is no reason why one sponsor should not take a number of offerings under their wing, as long as their detailed grip on each one of them is not impaired. A different case is that of the contract to build a nuclear power station. The company might have only this one offering, or only a handful of offerings. Such a company might of course need no sponsors, with each offering having its own line manager. However, if sponsors are needed, there will be one for each offering. The total number of sponsors in that company with few offerings will thus be equal to the number of offerings.

Should sponsors be specialists, for example in marketing, production or purchasing?

Here again the nature of the offerings can make a difference. If the offering is a pharmaceutical company's next new drug, the sponsor may well be a research chemist, but in the normal run of things they will not be a specialist at all. They have responsibilities for all aspects of an offering, for example external and internal aspects, and that normally requires a generalist. As one of the sponsor's principal tasks is to know and watch the customers and competitors, it might be thought that they need to be trained in marketing. Well, of course they would benefit from that training, but so would *any* general manager. They must, however, also be well versed in the company's winning and other resources, in purchasing, and in finance. They certainly need a thorough grasp of the concept of the cost of capital. So normally they should certainly not be a narrow specialist, but turn to functional experts for advice. Their own specialization needs to be in the offerings in their charge.

Is not the design of a new offering a specialized task?

Yes it is. It takes some unusual skills to design a new offering. However, the sponsor must, above all, be a manager rather than a specialist: they will call on others to help with specialised skills. Their function is the broad one of ensuring that the offering will achieve its purpose by building value in its private (or perhaps public) market.

When does the sponsor's task begin and end?

That task begins with the design of the offering and ideally ends only when the offering ceases to generate value and needs to be divested. To the very end the sponsor has to act as monitor.

Why is continuity needed between the design and the implementation stages?

Many people fail to see why these quite diverse tasks are best discharged by the same person. It seems inconsistent with the division of labour, under which each task is done by whoever does it best. The answer lies once again in the critical role of the customer. Few things alienate a customer more than to be confronted at the implementation stage with managers who are not even aware of the processes that led to the choice of us as supplier and of the commitments then made.

The engineering contract is of course the extreme example of an offering co-designed by the customer. How about a fast-moving consumer offering such as a vacuum cleaner where there is no personal relationship before the sale? Here the process is different, but continuity is still essential. When we designed the new model vacuum cleaner, we had to do much research into customer preferences and into the competing substitutes likely to be offered by competitors, about the price at which our offering would generate value. In that indirect and passive sense customers do therefore play a part in the design process. It is unlikely that our chosen design will build value if those responsible for its delivery are not intimately aware of just how it was designed to achieve that effect with customers, and with precisely which customer segments. Subsequent events may well compel changes in the offering, but they will also entail changes in costs and other implementation factors, and a single brain must integrate both sets of changes and relate them to the original concept.

Complete continuity from conception to death of the offering in all its changing forms may not always be achievable in a single person. That lifespan in the case of a nuclear power station or an aircraft like the Airbus A380 might be 20 or more years. The career of any one person with the same company may not span such a long period. That practical difficulty does not, however, change the principle. If there is an unavoidable succession in the sponsorship of an offering, the need is still for maximum continuity. The new sponsor needs to be as familiar as possible with the way in which the offering was designed to attract customers so as to build value. Nor will the practical issues normally be as difficult as in the nuclear power plant. Lifespans of offerings are typically shortening all the time.

Do companies structured by customer groups not meet the need for continuity?

The questioner might here have in mind, for example, a commercial bank with separate divisions for (i) individual and small business customers and (ii) corporate wholesale customers. Does not that structure meet the need for continuity without going to the length of sponsorship?

Well, large banks in Europe with that structure have in the past been notoriously lacking in attention to how customers compare their offerings with those of competitors. The focus on competitive positioning on how customers see the bank's offerings needs to be much more specific. Each offering needs separate attention. A structure with divisions representing different customer groups is at best a useful start towards meeting that requirement.

How do sponsors fit into management units?

Many offerings fit neatly into a single management unit, using no significant resources from other units. Many others are more interdependent with those other units.

Ideally the sponsor has no responsibilities other than their sponsored offerings. There are three main reasons for this:

- They have to fight their corner and to ensure that the resources are made available for their offerings. That would cause more jealousies and resistance if they had their own responsibilities for some resources, but not others.
- They need a mindset focused on market outcomes, free from conflicting internal preoccupations.
- They need to be *seen* as focused on outcomes, not as a rival by those charged with managing resources and assets in their own or other management units.

A sponsor will of course normally be subordinate to their unit manager, but not in the same chain of command as those responsible for resources and logistics. Moreover, as already said, some of their responsibilities are independent of the unit manager's. The presence of sponsors should give the whole unit a healthier balance between internal and market perspectives. In any case, the sponsor is often engaged in relations with other units that contribute to their offering.

The aim of leaving sponsors free from non-sponsoring commitments is of course a counsel of perfection. It is not always affordable. However, where sponsors are not fully stretched and have spare capacity, it may be preferable to have fewer sponsors with more offerings each, rather than to give them inward-looking control tasks. Moreover, where other units help to produce the offering, the less its sponsor is committed to just one of those units, the better.

If sponsors are not in charge of resources, how do they get empowered to obtain them for their offerings?

This is a key question, to which there is no simple clear answer, but which goes to the root of the conflict. Resources are commonly in short supply. Managers therefore have to allocate them, or compete for them if they are not under their own control. In complex companies there will be offerings for which no single manager is responsible. For example, there may be no single line manager whose task is to compete for the resources needed by a given offering. Our sponsor is responsible for all that.

The conflict is not *created* by our offering-centred structure with sponsors. On the contrary, it is inherent in the facts of business. Internal resource and asset structures can seldom follow the pattern of external customer markets or offerings in those markets. There are very few complex businesses where offerings use only their own separate resources, and do not share resources with other offerings. It is not even common for offerings to use exclusively resources located within their own management units. The facts of business are seldom that tidy, except in very simple or small businesses.

No question illustrates more sharply why sponsors are needed. Where resources are stretched, those in charge of them are subject to many pressures, most of them aimed at internal efficiencies. Without sponsors the needs of customers, or rather of the company's efforts to attract and serve profitable customers, are apt to take a back seat in setting priorities. The sponsor is a very necessary source of counter-pressure on behalf of customers and the need to serve them. At the implementation stage this is often the most important of the sponsor's tasks.

> You can have months on end when you don't think about strategy. . . . But you can't have a day when you aren't obsessed by operations, cash-generation and people (Roger Parry, head of the international arm of Clear Channel, in a book on the role of the CEO).[1]

The task causes two types of interface for the sponsor: one with the unit manager for resources controlled within the unit and another with other parts of the company for resources controlled outside that unit. In many cases a higher level of authority has to allocate resources between units. It is very necessary for the higher level to be customer-focused too, and sponsors will press for that.

Who Is Responsible for What?

We have here tackled the conflict between a unit structure largely shaped by internal control issues and an offering-centred view of business strategy. A full review of how responsibilities should be allocated at the four stages of strategy will be possible only after our review in Chapter 15 of how corporate strategy affects that allocation. The resulting picture is summarized in Table 15.1.

Summary

This chapter has looked at the conflict between unit structures driven by internal control issues and strategies for offerings driven by pressures from the external market, that is from customers and competitors. Many companies are complex enough for each offering to need a sponsor whose focus is on the external market. The benefit of this solution transcends issues of organization structure. It counteracts the predominant over-preoccupation with internal issues.

Note

1. Quoted in The Economist's survey of corporate leadership: Tough at the top. *The Economist*, 25 October 2003, p. 17.

15

Delivering value through corporate strategy

Introduction: Corporate Strategy Can be a Major Value-Builder

This chapter reviews the practical issues of formulating and implementing *corporate* strategies for *collections* of offerings. Here too the use of offerings as the unit of strategy makes a significant difference.

Our account of corporate strategy in Part 4 may raise some eyebrows. It does not advocate creating an ever larger, more diversified company. On the contrary, we stress the advantages of a simpler, more focused company that sticks to the few things it does best. Nor do we depict corporate strategy as a glamorous, dramatic process with takeover battles, 'white knights', management buyouts, or demergers: the stuff of newspaper headlines. The overwhelming majority of decisions are about small changes in the collection of offerings:

- a pharmacy becoming its own photographic processor;
- a builder and decorator deciding to stop offering paperhanging as part of his service;
- a bus company adding a café at its terminal;
- a dental practice employing a dental mechanic, located at its surgery;
- a chain such as Chili's deciding to open a restaurant in London's Canary Wharf; and
- Singer deciding to franchise the servicing of its sewing machines.

That is why throughout this book we stress the humdrum day-by-day search for value-building new offerings, most of them grown internally.

Above all we recommend continuous scanning of the collection for offerings to divest, by selling them or even by simply phasing them out when they cease to build value. Big, dramatic moves do play a part, but not the major part.

However, this humdrum, less exciting view of corporate strategy is far from small beer. Our company can generate enormous value by steadfastly building on its own strengths, and above all by correctly timing its divestments close to the point at which each offering ceases to build value. Nearly all companies keep offerings running far beyond that time, destroying value from then on. A company that manages to avoid that bloodletting will outperform most others. If that is an unexciting view of corporate strategy, it is nonetheless a rewarding one.

Structuring for Corporate Strategy

We now review the implications for corporate strategy of treating the offering as the strategic unit. Chapter 14 did this for competitive strategy.

Here too a distinctive contribution of this framework is what it does *not* say. We do not take a *general* view whether it is better to centralize or decentralize, or whether a divisional structure should be preferred to a functional structure and so on. Those issues are in our view a matter of horses for courses.

First, a majority of people do not work in giant companies, but in much smaller, perhaps owner-managed businesses, too simple to need divisions or even profit centres.

Secondly, even among large companies it is not sensible to advocate this type of structure or that without first having a look at what their business is. Mass production of consumer goods needs a very different structure from large-scale civil construction, which has a large and intensive interface with individual customers. A contractor for nuclear power plants or a major airframe manufacturer may need a much simpler structure than a steel company with many different offerings. Structure depends on the nature of the business.

Our review in Part 4 of corporate strategy did, however, note certain features which are worth recapitulating.

First, corporate strategy depends heavily on initiatives and proposals from managers close to the offerings. Chapter 14 suggested that these should be sponsors. On the other hand, approvals of new offerings and retain-or-divest decisions must be the task of top management: only top management has the information needed to assess how these proposals would affect the collection as a whole. At any subordinate level, the risk is that adverse repercussions for other management units will not receive adequate consideration. Top management must also keep under review larger issues, such as whether the company would be more valuable if it were smaller or more narrowly focused.

Second, in technically complex, opaque or long-fuze offerings the head office needs to be a more active participant in strategy-making even at grassroots level, because here it has to understand and manage the risks which those offerings carry; risks which financial markets cannot manage in a timely and adequate fashion. The head office here carries the function which financial markets discharge for ordinary offerings. This is why Link 7 in Chapter 12 is needed.

Third, the head office must in any case *understand* the significant risks of all offerings, significant enough to pose potentially serious threats to the company as a whole. Chapter 12 cited the example of free flights offered by Hoover's UK subsidiary. It showed that this need applies not just to technically complex, opaque or long-fuze offerings.

That need to understand the risks of all offerings applies much more intensively to a special class of offerings, which consist of accepting and managing customers' risks. Examples are insurance underwriters and also banks which make large loans or act as market makers in financial markets such as currencies or derivatives. These companies must centralize their structures considerably more than other companies, because otherwise (as Walter Wriston of Citicorp famously expressed it) a single dealer could 'bet the bank'.

The head office of a multi-offering company must ensure that sponsors and other managers close to the offerings think about new and successor offerings and make proposals for the head office to consider. The head office must also undertake a continuous scrutiny of the entire collection, so as to identify offerings ripe for divestment or replacement.

Corporate strategy is a continuous activity for the whole company, but with different tasks at the centre and at the coalface.

Analysing Proposals for New Offerings

We must here remember that any new or differently positioned toilet soap in our range is a new offering. As is an existing toilet soap brought to a new market like South Korea with different customer preferences or different competing substitutes. So too was the 'compact' edition of *The Times* which was at first in 2003 offered in addition to the editorially similar broadsheet edition, and then a year later replaced it altogether.

Analysing proposals for investment in new offerings is a special case of the wider and familiar task of evaluating any capital expenditure proposals. What is different here is the need to test for relatedness and to apply the three filters.

The suggested steps are the following:

- Check that the addition falls within one of the links of relatedness. If it does not, the proposal fails.
- Apply the three filters. If the proposal fails any one of them, it fails altogether.
- Embark on the better-off test by estimating the net effect of the addition of the new offering P on the company's entire annual cash flows over the entire payback period. This includes P's own cash flows and any plus or minus effects on cash flows elsewhere in the company. The new offering might, for example, cannibalise sales of other offerings, or make those offerings more attractive to customers.
- *Conservatively* estimate and allow for any option value inherent in P, that is the value of any opportunities to invest in other competitive strategies in the future: opportunities which would not exist without the addition of P to the collection.[1]
- Estimate – however broadly – the extra costs of diversified operation described in Chapter 13.
- Estimate the cost of internal investment or of acquisition (price and transaction costs), less cash proceeds of divestments of unwanted assets.
- Estimate any once-off restructuring costs.
- Estimate the risk-adjusted cost of capital of the proposal.

- Using all the above information, complete the better-off test, that is calculate the net effect of the proposal on the financial value of the company as a whole. For this purpose ascertain the NPV of the proposal from the sum of the incremental cash flows, discounted at the offering's cost of capital. The calculation must take account of any impact that the proposal may have on the entire company's investment rating, and cost of capital and also tax or other technical financial effects. If P took the company into gaming or betting, for example, the company's investment rating would surely decline, and its cost of capital rise. If the resulting NPV is still positive, the better-off test is passed.

Analysing Whether to Retain or Divest an Existing Offering

The retain-or-divest analysis is similar to the analysis of a proposed new offering, but the two tasks also differ in important respects. There are three important reasons for this:

1. *The time difference*: Suppose that offering O was planned in year −3, launched in year 0 and that we are now in year +3. Some of the most important uncertainties at year −3 are now historical facts. Its competitive positioning against customers and competitors, the cost structures and the financial performance to date, all these are now known with the precision of hindsight.
2. *O's remaining lifespan*: The present task is not to ascertain the value to be built by offering O over its entire life from year 0, but how much value it is expected to build *from now* in year +3. Now has become the base time. Will it add value for another 3 months, or another 3 years, or has it already ceased to build value? Even if it will only add value for another 3 months, we should ideally not divest now. This is why retention decisions do not need the robustness filter. The forward look is both shorter and less uncertain.
3. *Interdependence*: Offering O may have become too interdependent with other parts of our collection to be divestable on its own. Its divestment might stop other offerings P and Q building value. Perhaps O, P and Q share major fixed costs. That would be a supply

side reason. Or maybe customers would stop buying P and Q from us if we no longer sold O. That would be a demand side reason. A hotel might be unable to divest its conference business without also losing much of its banqueting and other turnover with business clients. Interdependence is not strictly confined to the retain-or-divest issue, but it is likely to be much more influential once an offering has been with us for some time. If P and Q are so interdependent with O that we can divest only all three or none, then the better-off test must be applied to the divestment of all three together.

The analysis must, as always, be in opportunity cost terms, against the best alternative course of action. This might, for example, be simply to discontinue the offering, or to sell it to a competitor, or to replace it with an updated and improved version.

To make it easy, we assume that we can divest O without having to divest P and Q as well. In that case the analysis might take the following sequence:

- Again test for relatedness and the two filters, market-instead and best-owner, before conducting the detailed analysis. It may save a lot of time and effort.
- Estimate net cash flows lost by divestment: O's cash flows plus the cash flows which our other offerings would lose, either by fixed costs no longer shared or by sales lost by our other offerings. However, some other offerings may for example gain extra customers.
- Estimate and allow for any option value inherent in O.
- Estimate company overheads to be saved. For example, if O is a significant part of the company, it may be possible to reduce the personnel department, the audit fee or space occupied.
- Estimate savings in costs of diversified operation. These costs are very hard to quantify, but some rough assessment is important if O accounts for a significant part of the total activity of the head office.
- Estimate the once-off costs of divestment, such as redundancy, real estate agents and restructuring costs.
- Estimate the capital released by the divestment, either by liquidation or by sale. Include the effect of tax and the possible use of tax-minimizing structures.

- Ascertain O's cost of capital and then from the above estimates calculate the NPV of the divestment. Remember that a divestment can affect the company's cost of capital and thus the discount rate, if financial characteristics like gearing or leverage of the balance sheet are changed.
- Check and adjust for any knock-on effect on the investment rating and thus the cost of capital of the rest of the company. For example, it might make the business less cyclical or shift it from one industrial classification to another in the view of the financial markets.
- If the offering is still adding value to the company, retain; otherwise divest.

Why Do We Need to Test an Existing Offering for Relatedness and Two of the Filters?

At first sight it may seem unnecessary to apply the tests for relatedness, market-instead and best-owner to an existing offering that had passed them when it was originally added. However, things may have changed in the meantime.

First, relatedness. For example, if O had been acquired for reasons of market power, because O and P together constituted a dominant power in the local pharmacy market, that market power could have been eroded since then by the local supermarkets entering the pharmacy business.

The market-instead filter too may be failed now, even though vertical integration was needed when O was originally added. There may have been a time when washing-machine manufacturers had cause to make their own motors for quality control reasons, but since then motors may have become so commoditized that internalization is no longer an advantage.

Again, since the best-owner filter was originally passed, a new competitor may have appeared with major advantages which now oust us from the position of best owner. About the turn of the millennium a number of international banks divested their custody offering to one of a few specialists such as the Bank of New York. This business clearly generated more value in that bank, which had better economies of scale in it.

This concludes what this chapter has to say about the analysis of specific decisions to add or divest offerings. We now turn to issues which arise at the implementation stage of a decision.

Bedding in a New Offering

Whenever we have a new offering in place, we need to ensure that it fits as well as possible into the collection as a whole. Very few new offerings have no effect on the rest of the company. The new offering may replace a previous one, it may use resources already supporting other offerings, it may introduce new or different risks that need managing, and above all it may make some other offerings either more or less attractive to customers. Those other offerings may or may not be within the same management unit as the new offering.

The new offering normally comes on stream some months or years after the decision to add it. The effects on other parts of the company – including in some cases the head office – should have been assessed at the time of that decision, but circumstances are only too likely to have changed. Now is the time to ensure that the new arrival has the best possible effect on the collection as a whole, and also that any fresh problems are dealt with before damage results. This is not normally a very burdensome task, but it is rare to find a company with a firm routine for discharging it. The rewards can be big, and so can the penalties for neglect.

Managing the Aftermath of Divestments

Is there a similar problem after an offering has been divested? There may well be cases where the divested offering is so insignificant in the total collection and so separate from the rest of the collection that little needs to be done after it has gone, but those cases may be rare. Most offerings affect the usage of resources, the cost structure and the attraction of other offerings to customers. The removal of some offerings provides an opportunity to reduce the overhead incurred by the head office.

Where there are significant links, the effects of the divestment must be managed in the transition phase. The unit costs or attractions of other offerings may have been adversely affected, and those adverse consequences must of course be minimized. Extra promotion expense may be needed. Steps may need to be taken either to reduce costs or to obtain extra volume for underutilized resources. Perhaps some new offerings are now desirable.

Whether these issues are critical depends on how large a gap the divested offering leaves, but in any event they too need attention at the earliest practical time if value is not to be lost or wasted.

Restructuring Acquisitions

Restructuring acquisitions is a special but prominent instance of the bedding-in task just described. Although acquisitions represent a minority of corporate strategy decisions, they are nevertheless a significant feature of corporate strategy. Among other things, they have a disproportionate impact on the company's standing in its financial markets. The track record is generally indifferent, for many reasons. One of those is that too many members of the small team that plans an acquisition have no adequate plans for restructuring the acquired businesses. This task needs to be planned well before the event.[2]

To begin with, it is almost impossible to acquire just what we want. If we want offerings P and Q, an acquisition will almost inevitably give us further offerings which we did not want, and which would not pass the condition of relatedness, or the better-off test, or the filters. Hence we need to redivest them, and probably quite swiftly before they lose more value in our hands. This is not to deny the need for opportunism and for good timing, or other opportunities to make the unwanted offerings leaner and fitter before divestment, but neither should we lose more value than we might save by waiting for a better price.

However, even the activities we wanted to acquire will almost certainly need to be restructured. They may need changes of reporting relationships, possibly of management and sometimes of location, if we are to realize the benefits of relatedness with our existing collection. Urgent attention is also needed to operating systems and routines, information systems and management incentives. That last point is critical if we are not to lose the key people we need to retain. The best people are likely to be the most marketable ones.

The need to reconfigure the new offerings arises not just in terms of operating inputs, but even more in terms of outputs for customers. A new offering in our collection may either attract customers to our existing offerings or repel them. The new structure must get the best possible overall effect for the company, and that needs reconnaissance and acumen.

Successful acquisitions are rare. The few exceptions are likely to be those where all these matters are sorted out without delay, and with the shortest possible learning curve. The acquirer needs to have a set of policies and a skilled restructuring team ready on day 1. The acquired units can easily disintegrate if exposed to more than the absolute minimum of unsettling uncertainty.

Restructuring is a discrete, one-off creation of value. However, a good-related acquisition often requires an *additional* longer-term process of value creation.[3] This longer-term effort welds two or more businesses together, brings capabilities to bear on the partner that has not yet enjoyed their benefits and generally ensures that the potential benefits of the merger are achieved. Corporate strategy has to focus very directly and persistently on the aim of value creation.

Corporate and Competitive Strategy: Who Does What in Complex Companies?

Corporate strategy and competitive strategy are not in conflict. Both seek to improve the value of the company by adding value-building offerings. However, they approach that aim from different perspectives. Competitive strategy is focused on one offering at a time, corporate strategy on the company as a whole and its collection of offerings. Their tasks are different, but they overlap and interact.

The interface between the two tasks mainly concerns the position of sponsors in the structure. The CEO and the head office of a complex company should not normally have day-to-day supervision of sponsors. Their task is to ensure that sponsors are in place in the various management units, and given the authority they need to do their jobs effectively.

There is in most businesses a tendency to focus on internal efficiency, if only because that is the line of least resistance. Roger Parry was quoted on this in a text-box in Chapter 14. Internal issues are

Table 15.1 Who is responsible at various stages?

	Corporate strategy	Competitive strategy
Designed by	CEO	Sponsor
Approved by	CEO	CEO
Implemented by	CEO's appointee	Sponsoring unit manager and sponsor
Monitored by	CEO or appointee	Sponsor

controllable, customers and competitors are not. Hence unit managers will not always naturally welcome the pressures that come from sponsors. A good head office will watch and correct that tendency. In some cases it may be desirable for CEOs to appoint the sponsors, without, however, also taking on their day-to-day supervision. The strains and stresses that may result are not due to the existence of sponsors, but inherent in the nature of business itself.

Divestments are an important potential source of strain. Competitive strategy aims to create new offerings, corporate strategy has the vital function of terminating them when they no longer build value. Sponsors have to share in this task of corporate strategy. This can add tension between them and their unit managers. Again a good CEO and head office will ensure that this tension works beneficially for the company.

Finally, and most importantly, a good head office will communicate clearly how strategic issues fit into the organization structure. Table 15.1 suggests how this might look.

The CEO in a company with more than a few offerings may need to delegate some implementation and monitoring tasks regarding corporate strategy to the 'appointees' in the table. These may be in the head office or in the operating units, but act on the CEO's personal behalf for this purpose. They must report to him or her when acting in that capacity. This task cannot normally be delegated to divisional heads, who tend to have strong commitments to their own patches.

Summary

This chapter has discussed some of the practical decision processes, structure and management issues of corporate strategy. It has set out the respective tasks of the head office and of sponsors and other managers close to the offerings and their customers. It has also discussed the important issues of bedding down new offerings and restructuring acquisitions. One of the most important issues is the need for changes in the collection to be planned before the event, and then sorted out as fast as possible after it, if value is not to be lost. A second one is the allocation of responsibilities between the head office and the operating units. Finally there are the tensions between inward-looking unit managers and customer-focused sponsors, and what role the head office may play in holding the balance.

Our account of corporate strategy differs from others in that it presents it in terms of offerings, not management units. That is why it stresses the role of sponsors. None of this diminishes the personal responsibility for corporate strategy of the CEO and his or her top team.

Notes

1. Kester, W.C. (1984). Today's options for tomorrow's growth. *Harvard Business Review*, March–April, pp. 153–160.
2. Hubbard, N. (2001). *Acquisition: Strategy and Implementation.* Basingstone: Palgrave.
3. Haspeslagh, P.C. and Jemison, D.B. (1991). *Managing Acquisitions: Creating Value through Corporate Renewal.* New York: Free Press.

PART 6

Final Reflections

Part 6 consists of one chapter. It looks back over the offering-based framework for competitive and corporate strategy presented in the book. It highlights those features that managers are likely to find most irksome and sheds light on the causes of these tensions. It suggests that once these reasons are understood the importance of these features in improving a manager's grip on strategy becomes even more obvious.

16

Stumbling-blocks and entrenched attitudes

Introduction

Practical managers tend to find our framework for competitive and corporate strategy attractive. At the same time some of its fundamental features are at odds with many managers' entrenched attitudes to running a business. We have drawn attention to those stumbling-blocks throughout the book: in this chapter we revisit them.

Our aim in homing in on these tough features in our framework is to explain why they are sometimes resisted, why they are nevertheless needed for better strategy-making and what we can profitably learn from all this. This should help those who wish to test-drive our model, because it warns against attempts to bypass or ignore these features. Some disappointments will be avoided, because the urge to downplay or resist these stumbling-blocks is precisely what has caused so many past failures.

Above all, this review of the stumbling-blocks should improve awareness of what improvements in mindsets are most likely to improve performance. If these features were more widely accepted, there should be a lot fewer failures.

Here are the stumbling-blocks:

1. focus on value rather than size or growth as the purpose of business;
2. focus on individual offerings;
3. focus on external forces: customers and competitors;

4. focus in competitive strategy on non-head office issues;
5. focus on the scissors with two blades requiring both a winning competitive position and also the use of winning resources; and
6. focus on divesting offerings which have ceased to build value.

We shall discuss each stumbling-block under three heads:

a. Causes: Why is it resisted, yet needed?
b. Categories: To what extent is this stumbling-block a feature of large or small, or simple or complex businesses?
c. Lessons: How can we make the resisted feature work for us?

The heads (a) and (c) explain the stumbling-block and draw practical lessons from it. Head (b) explores the extent to which the stumbling-block is peculiar to large, small, simple or complex businesses.

As explained in Chapter 1, we call a 'complex' business one that needs both top and senior middle managers, some of whom are not directly concerned with customers and offerings. Businesses which are not complex, we call 'simple'. A 'small' business we define as one too small to need any specialized management. Those which do need specialized management we call 'large', but a large business need not be complex. If the sole activity of a business is to build a nuclear power plant, it may have no senior managers who are not concerned with that offering and its customer, but it may nevertheless need at least junior specialized managers. These distinctions may help us to get a better understanding of the stumbling-blocks. That is true despite a substantial overlap. It is hard to think of a small company which is not also simple, but not hard at all to find companies which are simultaneously large and simple.

1: Focus on Value, Rejecting Size as an End in Itself

Causes

Our framework in this book rejects size as an end in itself. The full case for that rejection is argued in Chapter 2. This stumbling-block challenges a deeply entrenched mindset. Our rejection of size is not just philosophical. It has at least three practical applications. First, we insist that the test for accepting an offering is financial value, not size. The test is not whether it increases our sales, our market share, our global reach, our balance sheet or even our market capitalization, but whether it has a positive NPV, and thus boosts financial value. Anyone who has experienced a takeover threat knows that this is what counts. Second, our stress on related diversification and on the better-off test and the filters focuses strategy on value-building investments. Third, we stress the need to divest offerings that no longer build value. In many companies that alone would substantially improve results.

Admittedly, resistance to the single objective of financial value is also in many companies fed by other hang-ups such as a nostalgic attachment to present offerings, or sheer inertia, but worship of size is arguably the biggest source of failure.

Chapter 2 made the case that the purpose of business is to build financial value. It showed that there is no necessary connection between financial value and size, not even if by size we mean financial size. A company can increase its market capitalization and in the process reduce its financial value, making itself more vulnerable to takeover. An example might be an unfortunate acquisition, or a disastrous investment project. The requirement of relatedness, set out in Chapter 12, disqualifies many unrelated diversification proposals which would undoubtedly make the company bigger.

Categories

Is the cult of size rifer in some kinds of companies than in others?

Comparing small with large businesses

Many small businesses are still in their start-up phase, and need to grow in order to realize economies of scale. At that stage size is often a value-builder, as long as its pursuit is single-mindedly aimed at scale economies.

Start-ups apart, even small companies need to be watchful against the temptation to pursue size. Unfortunately there is no reason to believe that those who run small businesses are less vulnerable to the lure of size than those who run large companies. The temptation certainly exists in all large companies.

Comparing simple with complex businesses

We have noted that a simple business can be large, as long as it has only a handful of offerings. Thus a bus company in a large city might simply have a general passenger service, a service for schoolchildren, a parcels service and private coach hire: four activities in all. Similarly an automobile manufacturer might only have three or four models.

Is the simple company less tempted than the complex company to go for size rather than financial value? Not in principle. In practice, the answer may turn on why the simple company is simple:

- If the company is simple *by design*, then its CEO is unlikely to stray from the chosen path and go for size.
- If, on the other hand, the company is simple because it is still in its start-up phase, then it may well need to grow in any case, for non-doctrinal reasons. In a start-up phase economies of scale are often underexploited.
- Where the company is simple for neither of those two reasons, its managers are just as likely to have the growth bug as those of a complex company.

Complex companies all appear to be vulnerable to this temptation.

The preoccupation with size therefore seems to affect all four categories of companies: small, large, simple and complex. On the other hand, it may not be harmful in start-ups.

Lessons

This is simply a case of the right mindset, particularly for the CEO. Where diversification proposals are generated at other levels, the CEO should educate other managers in the reasons for rejecting the aim of size and pursuing value instead.

2: Focus on Offerings

Undoubtedly many managers find it hard to accept our focus on offerings and our treatment of the offering as the strategic unit.

Causes

What is the difficulty? Offerings are usually too small and too numerous to be a convenient unit for control. Offerings are nonetheless the critical units for strategy. This book has stressed that again and again. The offering is what customers choose, and what must therefore be designed for competitive success. A customer chooses tennis balls, not sports goods. Sports goods as a category or even as a brand has no price that customers can compare with competing prices. An offering needs to be designed and planned with the object of being chosen by enough customers for long enough to beat the cost of capital. We may need to make decisions about more than one offering at a time, but each has to be *designed* separately, because its competitive position vis-à-vis customers and competitors is unique. This is one of this book's principal messages.

Categories

Is the central place of the offering more resisted in some kinds of businesses?

Comparing small with large businesses

In a small business like that of a shoe repairer the focus on offerings is unavoidable. An owner who also sells shoe polishes and brushes, laces, or even footwear or luggage cannot help thinking in terms of the various offerings. The capacity of the business to build value could clearly be affected by any change in the range of offerings. The critical point here is not the range or its diversity, but the fact that a single person is in charge of strategy, sales, procurement, staffing and finance.

In large, but simple businesses the focus on offerings will also be natural, as the same people take the decisions about offerings and internal matters like facilities, costs and staffing.

Comparing simple with complex businesses

Would the difficulty arise in a simple business? No. The CEO of a simple business would of necessity be sensitive to the preferences of customers in the market of each offering. This stumbling-block characterizes the complex business, no matter whether the business is small or large.

Lessons

For the complex business this is a central problem, discussed in Chapter 14. Briefly, a single offering seldom makes a natural management unit, such as an SBU or a division, yet needs the attention, the responsibility and the continuity of attention and responsibility of a single manager. Our suggestion for resolving this inherent tension is to appoint a sponsor.

3: Focus on External Forces: Customers and Competitors

Our focus on customer markets, and thus on external parties is shared by marketing people, but not always by other managers.

Causes

Managers have major control responsibilities for employees, resources and costs. These preoccupations are immediate, constant and unavoidable. They naturally generate an inward-facing mindset which does not easily or naturally extend to uncontrollable external forces. Yet it is those external forces that present the company with its strategic task. It is in this external environment that our internal resources must create value. Control faces inwards, strategy outwards. Customers are the people whose decisions determine our success or failure. Competitors' moves determine the options open to our customers. There is no cutting-edge science behind either of these facts: what hides them from view is not logic, but the daily grind of controlling our own operations, especially in the complex business.

Categories

Is our focus on customer markets a greater problem in some businesses than in others?

Comparing small with large businesses

A small business is likely to be simple: a single manager is likely to combine the marketing and control functions. If so, the conflict between their respective problems disappears. The single manager has little opportunity to forget the need to succeed in the market.

If a large company is so simple that a single manager combines the marketing and control functions, this conflict will again be absent.

Comparing simple with complex businesses

Clearly, the conflict will not occur in simple companies, but the complex company is precisely where this stumbling-block is apt to be a problem.

It is again the complex company where we are likely to encounter resistance to a focus on customers. The company's size is not what matters.

Lessons

If our business is complex, then the appointment of sponsors will tend to solve this problem too. Customers and competitors are the environment in which offerings have to succeed. The sponsor who in a complex business is charged with the success of the offering cannot do her job without this focus. Moreover in such a company sponsors may well turn out to be the only people with that focus.

4: Focus on Non-Head Office Issues in Competitive Strategy

This stumbling-block affects outsiders more than insiders in a business. Strategy is widely assumed to be about the things that top managers handle directly. Some central features of our framework are not invariably handled at the top.

Causes

Our framework is based on offerings, and we suggest that in complex companies offerings need to be designed by people closer to customers and markets than the CEO can normally be. Few CEOs have a sufficiently intimate grasp of the markets in which each present and future offering has to succeed. This requires a close familiarity with customers and competitors and with changes in the configuration of these market participants.

The CEO or chairman may therefore lack a sufficient grasp of the main issues of competitive strategy to answer questions by journalists and analysts who are the eyes and ears of the financial markets, or by shareholders attending the annual general meeting. This goes against the convenience of those markets. Financial markets expect the Chairman and CEO to be able to answer questions about strategic intents concerning competitive issues. This expectation may be unrealistic, but that does not remove the awkwardness. If a CEO, when questioned, for example, at a press conference, is seen to lack familiarity with these customer market issues, the financial market may lose some of its confidence in that CEO's competence. In our view, the financial markets would be wrong to take that view. There are, however, signs that they do in fact take it. Conglomerates have, since about 1980, lost some of their investment status, and this may have been a contributory factor.

It is not only financial markets that find it convenient to deal with top managers on questions of strategy. It is also true of consultants and many researchers. For all these reasons strategy is widely thought of as a top-level issue. Writers on management have not done much to dispel that impression.

Offerings are of course a strategic issue for the head office, in the sense that every addition or divestment of an offering needs central approval. The offering may affect other offerings not managed by the sponsoring unit. If we stop offering tennis balls, we may lose sales of tennis rackets. However, the *design* of a new offering needs to be the task of people closer to its intended customers and competitors. This need is in our view so great that it outweighs the awkwardness of losing intimate familiarity with competitive strategic issues at the top level. If financial markets dislike it, they would do better to direct their criticism at complexity itself.

Categories

This book gives prominence to issues of competitive strategy which are not always handled at the top. Does this cause more difficulty in some businesses than in others?

Comparing small with large businesses

The small company has no hierarchical management structure with a separate head office. Hence the design and approval of a new offering are in the same hands. This stumbling-block does not therefore affect it.

In the large, but simple business too there is no head office separate from managers who design a new offering. Consequently, here again there is no conflict and no stumbling-block. Strategic thinking about offerings here is not located below the level of a head office.

Comparing simple with complex businesses

Conflict is, however, generated in the complex business. As long as a business is simple, the design of offerings does not take place at a subordinate level. The CEO knows the offerings and its customers. Hence the CEO can confidently communicate with investors, brokers and others in the financial markets about competitive strategy. This stumbling-block too therefore is a feature of the complex business.

The complex business needs a separate head office which approves offerings designed at a lower level. The stumbling-block therefore in practice affects only complex companies. Simple companies do not need a separate head office.

As with stumbling-blocks 2 and 3, our focus on non-head office issues causes difficulty only in complex businesses. The size of the business is not what matters.

Lessons

Good strategy formulation is not easy in the complex company. The difficulties stem from the nature of such a company. To make this focus on non-head office issues work for us, we need not just sponsors, but a flexible and dynamic organization structure which enables sponsors to report to their unit managers for day-to-day operational and implementation matters, but also to top management for strategic decisions. Chapter 14 discusses the tensions which this creates, and how best to manage them.

This stumbling-block serves to bring one conflict to a head. The complex company has in effect to choose between giving analysts and journalists easy access to its strategic thinking, and designing good strategies. It cannot do both. Something must give, and that has to be easy access to the financial market's eyes and ears. This is one of the penalties of complexity. Investors must presumably prefer difficult communication to poor strategies. Access to information is not blocked, just a little less convenient.

5: Focus on Both Blades of the Scissors

We stress that a winning offering needs both a winning competitive position and at least one winning resource. This is unpopular with those looking for a single cause and remedy for every problem. It also offends extreme standard bearers of the marketing and resources schools.

Causes

Many managers, but also, many writers believe that success depends on some single main factor. There is an element of wishful thinking here. Views differ on what that single factor might be. The touchstone for successful strategy may be imagined to lie in a variety of single factors such as cost, good organization, technical superiority, meeting customers' requirements or preferences, or market share. Some of these are on the supply side, others on the demand side. To be fair, few people believe that their preferred single factor is the only one that matters. For example, no manager is naïve enough to think that costs need not be competitive. However, many believe that some single feature is decisive. The biggest divide is between some marketing people who believe that success with customers or in growing market share alone can ensure the creation of value, and those who believe that the deployment of superior resources on its own can do that.

We firmly believe that both requirements are essential, one on the demand and one on the supply side. The first is a winning competitive position, the other the deployment of one or more winning resources. The first requires our offering to be so placed against competing substitutes that sufficient customers choose it at a price/volume combination that beats our cost of capital. The second requires us to use some skill or other asset which distinguishes our company from its competitors, and is needed to maintain superior returns for the offering during the whole of its payback period. Success can only come where we can outdo our rivals.

The most brilliant resource will not build value unless the offering is attractive enough to customers. Similarly, the best competitive position cannot successfully defeat onslaughts from competitors, unless we are uniquely placed to occupy and retain that superior position for the whole of the payback period. That is why both are needed.

Categories

Does our two-blade framework raise more eyebrows in some types of companies than in others?

Whereas our previous last three stumbling-blocks are prevalent in complex businesses, a conscious recognition that both these blades of the scissors are needed is unknown in just about any business. The small, large, simple and complex categories do not appear to be relevant in this case. There is little point in analysing the incidence of this stumbling-block separately for the four categories of businesses.

Managers of simple and small companies are more likely to be aware of the needs of both the demand and the supply side. However, for strategy a mere awareness of both sides is not enough. What is needed for the success of a planned offering is both a *winning* competitive position and the use of a *winning* resource. It needs a potentially value-building market area and our company's very own excellence. That recognition goes against the instincts of those not trained in the logic of competitive markets. It needs the insight that every advantage attracts competitive counterforces which seek to imitate or appropriate that advantage. Without that recognition, people tend to resist the twin requirement, because it seems to make the task harder for no apparent reason.

Hence this stumbling-block cannot be ascribed to any one of our four categories.

Lessons

This question is a tough one. We can only make this issue work for us by becoming better informed about the market forces faced by each offering. In other words here we simply need better management education. That answer always risks being taken for a cop-out, like a recommendation to be 'against sin'. It is above all a case for thoughtfulness and for reflecting on the nature and purpose of competitive business. Thoughtful literature or courses on the purpose and theory of business and business strategy can help here. Perhaps the main lesson is to resist the lure of simplistic panaceas, however fashionable and however superficially attractive. Strategy is not simple. If it were, there would be far fewer failures.

6: Focus on Divesting Offerings that no Longer Build Value

The need to weed out yesterday's winners is not a new insight, but has long been a major stumbling-block in corporate strategy.

Causes

It is strange that this remains a stumbling-block in the twenty-first century. Since the 1980s, many companies have openly reduced their activities to a 'core' or focused collection, by selling, demerging or simply closing down not only what was no longer value-generating, but also whatever was not regarded as a core activity. Thus ICI in 1993–99 spun off its pharmaceutical division Zeneca, and set about concentrating its collection on specialty offerings, coatings and materials, and divesting its businesses in industrial chemicals. Similarly P&O's CEO about 2004 recognized that container ports had replaced its original 'core' business of operating ferries as its opportunity to create value.

There has been quite a vogue for divestment. However, it has not spread to all or perhaps even most companies. Perhaps the cult of size is so ingrained that only a minority of business leaders have so far outgrown it.

We are here concerned with the most obvious reason for divestment. No offering generates value for ever. There comes a point at which its returns decline to less than the cost of capital, and where it begins to lose value for the company and needs to be divested or replaced. The logic is as clear-cut and as inevitable as that.[1]

Categories

Is divestment more resisted in some types of business than in others?

Comparing small with large businesses

The small company may not have many offerings to divest, but its offerings are not immortal either. They too will one day reach their sell-by dates. So in principle the need to divest or replace applies equally to the small company. Is divestment a greater or lesser stumbling-block for such a company? This may be a close call. On the one hand, the small business should be more aware of the loss of value from an offering that has been kept on too long. On the other hand, the owner manager may be more sentimentally attached to each of the offerings than the CEO of a larger company. Hanging on too long to the business created by Daddy has ruined many families and frustrated Daddy's illusion of having bequeathed enduring prosperity to the next generation.

A large business, even if it is simple, may be more mature, more professionally managed than a small business, and its managers may be more attuned to the requirements of the financial markets. In many cases they may therefore be a little less sentimental about existing offerings and more alive to the need to build value.

Comparing simple with complex businesses

A single non-performing offering is likely to be more of a thorn in the managers' and owners' side in the simple than in the complex company. In the latter a single offering may not loom so large.

To sum up, resistance to divestment may well be somewhat rifer in small and simple businesses, but the worship of size causes resistance in all categories of companies.

Lessons

Correct divestment or replacement requires a mindset which accepts the need for it and the skill and discipline of getting the timing and assessment right, as set out in Chapter 13. The benefits of well-timed divestment can be substantial when compared with the normal tendency to keep offerings beyond the point at which they begin to lose value. Many offerings simply need to be replaced. They need either upgrading or repositioning in the light of moves by competitors or shifts in the preferences of customers.

A new discipline ensuring good timing of divestments near the point at which they cease to build value can hugely improve a company's performance. Complex companies need sponsors to help implement this.

Which Categories Cause Problems?

Our review can be broadly summed up in Table 16.1.

Our main discovery is that stumbling-blocks 2, 3 and 4 represent features which are most needed and most resisted in complex companies. The cause in all three cases is our focus on offerings and their customers and competing substitutes. The other three stumbling-blocks are resisted in all categories. The minor exception is that resistance to divestments may be slightly greater in small and simple companies.

Table 16.1 How categories of businesses affect the prevalence of each stumbling-block

Stumbling-block	Resisted in which categories (large, small, complex, simple)?
1 Size not end in itself	All categories, but harmless in start-ups
2 Focus on single offerings	Complex companies
3 Focus on outside parties	Complex companies
4 Focus on non-HO issues	Complex companies
5 Twin blades of scissors	All categories almost universally
6 Stress on divestments	All categories, but especially small and simple ones

Advantages of the Simple Company

A principal result of our examination of the six stumbling-blocks points to the advantages of the simple company. The simple company practically eliminates three of our stumbling-blocks. In the simple company the top manager or team takes strategic decisions about offerings and also has to fund the investment and deal directly with the funding market. The same person or team is directly concerned with both the financial markets and the commercial markets of the offerings, as well as with implementing the strategies. Figure 16.1 illustrates this.

That unity is what is lacking in the complex company. Figure 16.2 illustrates this. In the complex company there is a CEO and a head

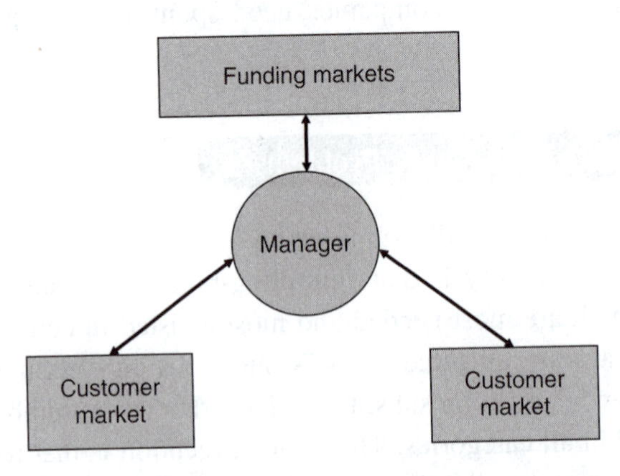

Figure 16.1 Simple company

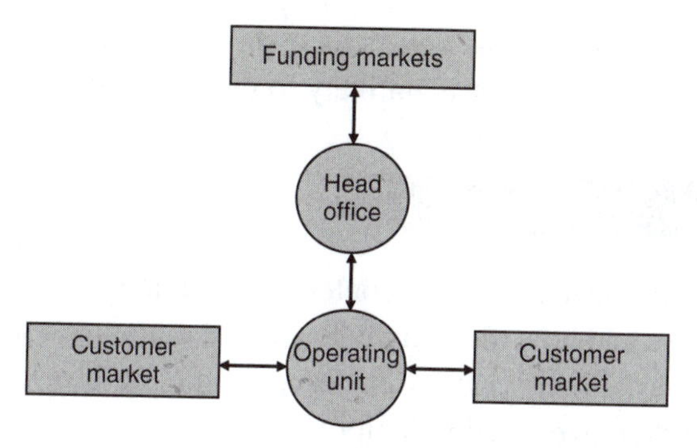

Figure 16.2 Complex company

office which sets overall objectives and has funding responsibility, and there are subordinate line managers who are in direct touch with the competitive markets in which each offering has to build value. That separation of functions causes three of our stumbling-blocks.

The simple company's top management can formulate competitive strategies for its few offerings. Top managers are close enough to customers and competitors to have a feel for the competitive positioning of those few offerings. They do not need sponsors or other subordinate managers to do that part of the task. In the complex company the head office still has to approve new offerings, but it cannot design them or assess their prospects. Similarly, it must approve divestments of offerings, but it cannot by itself assess their prospects of building value for the company.

The simple company has other advantages. First, complexity tends to dilute awareness at the lower levels of the overarching aim of financial value. The second advantage is the inherent relatedness of its collection of offerings. Investors have good reason to prefer simple companies. Hence they require a lower return on capital from simple companies. However, that is a symptom rather than the cause. The cause is that even CEOs are not universal geniuses. Top managers are unlikely to be as effective outside their own area of business as within it. Those who know how to make and sell tennis balls may not be the best people to run a pharmaceutical company. The issue here is the skills and competence of top management, the head office, not of the operating units. Wal-Mart may acquire Chase Manhattan and retain its managers, but it is unlikely that its head office will be as competent to run that bank as was its own head office. In any case an extra layer of management is unlikely to enhance value.

Summary and Conclusion

This chapter has listed the more contentious features in this framework, why they arise and how they might be applied to improve performance.

We have asked to what extent each stumbling-block is a consequence of either size or complexity.

Three of the stumbling-blocks are a result of complexity. Complexity here means that the responsibilities for initiating and taking material decisions are split between different organizational levels. Top management is not normally close enough to the customer market to design new offerings. Yet top management must understand and approve proposed additions, retention or divestments, and conduct relations with funding markets. This is a damaging drawback of complexity. Nor is it the only drawback. The worst of the other drawbacks is the extra costs of diversified operation, as we call them in Chapter 13. This chapter has suggested that complexity also distracts managers away from the essential logic of business success.

The other three stumbling-blocks are not significantly related to specific categories. The drive for size, the search for a single panacea and the reluctance to divest are all deeply ingrained attitudes. They can only be overcome by sober reflection on past business failures, and on the nature and purpose of business and its financial and competitive markets, and on the conditions of independent survival.

This book hopes to have shown the way to success, without wishful thinking, but with a focus on what customers want and what each business is really good at providing. The scissors framework does justice to the difficulties of creating value, but it does also point the way to achieving that elusive goal: valuable business strategy.

Note

1. It is remarkable how little attention is paid in marketing texts to divestment decisions, but see Kotler, P. (1965). Phasing out weak products. *Harvard Business Review*, March–April, pp. 107–118.

Index